*My Road Goes Ever On
Spiritual Being
Human Journey*

2nd Edition

Hardcover edition
A. K. Frailey

ISBN: 979-8-9944110-8-7

Copyright A. K. Frailey 2021
All rights reserved. No portion of this book may be reproduced in any form without permission from the publisher, except as permitted by U.S. copyright law. For permissions, contact akfrailey@yahoo.com.

Website https://akfrailey.com/

Amazon Author Page https://www.amazon.com/A.-K.-Frailey/e/B006WQTQCE

Cover Photo https://pixabay.com/photos/sky-tree-hill-sunset-nature-3189347/

A. K. Frailey Books

THE WRITINGS OF A. K. FRAILEY
Books for the Mind and Spirit

https://akfrailey.com/

Contemporary Literary Fiction
OLDTOWN Fly, Sparrow, Fly
OLDTOWN Brothers Born

Historical Science Fiction Novels
OldEarth ARAM Encounter
OldEarth Ishtar Encounter
OldEarth Neb Encounter
OldEarth Georgios Encounter
OldEarth Melchior Encounter

Science Fiction Novels
Homestead
Last of Her Kind
Newearth Justine Awakens
Newearth A Hero's Crime
Newearth Progeny
Newearth Relevance

Short Stories
It Might Have Been—And Other Short Stories 2nd Edition
One Day at a Time and Other Stories
Spice of Life and Other Stories
Encounter Science Fiction Short Stories & Novella 2nd Edition

Inspirational Non-Fiction
*The Road Goes Ever On: A Christian Journey Through
The Lord of the Rings*
*My Road Goes Ever On: Spiritual Being, Human Journey
2nd Edition*
My Road Goes Ever On: A Timeless Journey
My Road Goes Ever: On Rise Again

Children's Book
The Adventures of Tally-Ho
Wise Home
Wise Home on Lily Pad Pond

Poetry
Hope's Embrace & Other Poems 2nd Edition

**Audible Versions Available.
Check book details on Amazon
for current listings.**

Contents

Introduction	5
Joy and the Art of Contentment	6
On His Toes –	7
Life in Hollywood in the Early Days	7
The Stuff of Life	9
Rather Like Poetry	11
Homeschooling	13
J. R. R. Tolkien	15
Angels	17
Music	18
Mortal Eyes	19
Home Management	20
A Deeply Disturbed Ocean	21
A World Worth Saving	23
What Makes Heroes So Heroic?	25
Eight Kids and Grateful	26
Lenten Faith	28
You Converted Him—Right?	30
Untutored Wisdom	31
Gardening Grace	33
Interior Life	35
Simple Summer	37
Acceptance	38
A Change of Perspective	40
When a Leaf Falls	42
Love Is Life	44
A Culture of Encounter	46
Encounter Culture	48
The Blessed	50
Life in Lent	51
Hero's Quest	53
Real World Disconnect	54

Prayer, Work, Study	56
The Million-Faceted Crystal	58
Two Brains in One and Sleep Deprivation	59
Sunrise Paradox	61
My Kind of Madness	62
Turning Points	65
Picture Perfect	66
In a Wider Universe	67
Blanket Personalities	69
Love	71
Should Old Acquaintance Be Forgot	72
Human Journey	74
Getting Educated	76
No Guts, No Glory	78
This Side of the Divide	79
Some Days I Wonder	81
A Deep Moral Dilemma	84
Beyond Words	87
Surprise Me	89
Walk On Water	91
Well Lived	93
Ironic Twist of Fate	95
What Are We Searching For?	97
Brave Smile	99
Looking On the Bright Side	101
In the Souls of Those I Love	103
Go Get 'Em, Girl	105
I May Never Know Why	107
To believe in god	111
A Timeless Truth	113
Supernatural Synchronization	115
A New Heart	117
A Better Point	119
Learn As I Go	121
Another Season	124
Along the Roadside	126

Love Anyway	129
Whispering In My Ear	131
Living Spring Time	133
On Both Sides of the Road	136
The Real Reason	139
Take It Easy and Get Back to Work	141
Allow My Soul to Soar	143
Stars Twinkle in Concert with Darting Fireflies	145
What God Has Desired	148
Wisdom Between Them	151
A World of Faces	154
Make One Strong	156
Back to Shore	159
What Hope Looks Like	162
Love Alone	164
Tomorrow Is Another Day	166

We are not human beings having a spiritual experience.

We are spiritual beings having a human experience.

~Pierre Teilhard de Chardin

Introduction

Organizing has always been a pleasure of mine. Something I can control in a very uncertain world. When I decided to "organize" my blog posts, little did I know what I was getting into. I ran into what goes first in terms of first and second editions, putting work into chronological order, adapting kindle to paperback—and dealing with the unfortunate fact that page breaks and page numbers do not play well together.

But I have gained a lot from the experience overall. In reviewing my early work and moving into my later posts, I expected to see measurable growth. In the course of nearly ten years, I must have changed, right? Developed as a person. After all, my husband, several friends, and two brothers have died in the course of those years. The world suffered a pandemic. Good golly, the whole human race has endured fantastic trials in the last few years. I must be a better person for it, right?

I hope so. But in reality, I am still me. My core has remained much the same. I have certainly experienced a great deal of pain and joy, disaster and triumph, but the person that makes me—me remains much the same. And now I see that as a good thing.

I have gotten to know myself on deeper levels and learned to trust my intuition and judgment. I am both the same Ann Kristin Frailey, yet a better-informed, perhaps a more completely formed, version of myself. I certainly understand page breaks better. And they don't freak me out like they used to.

Joy and the Art of Contentment
Originally published on The Writings of A. K. Frailey 4/26/2012

Too often I find that I am waiting for this or that to happen, and then I'll give myself permission to be happy and know true contentment. Time passes and I get things on my to-do list finished just in time to fill up another list. It is like the laundry; I have finally accepted the fact that the laundry is never really done—it's just a cycle that goes around and around and around.

But life is more than laundry or jobs or things that must be dealt with. If that is all God wanted from us then He would have done better to make us robots. But he didn't. He risked our immortal souls by giving us free wills, which allows us to know Him intimately or reject Him utterly. God is willing to live with us and die for us. That truth makes my particular to-do list rather insignificant by comparison.

Don't get me wrong. I love to achieve results: keep the house clean, teach the kids, organize and plan with the best of moms, but I know that the temptation to work without reference to the God who made me is very great. I end up thinking that disasters like a spoiled dinner, a ruined shirt, or a torn book make the world less good. Or when I set goals that are not achieved as quickly as I would like, the sun doesn't seem to shine so brightly.

Yet God exists even when real disasters strike, and I can always love Him. In that acceptance, I feel a joy of contentment because my worth is not based on a thing or a result but on the desire of my God, who made me on purpose for some definite good.

So, I once again sally forth to take a walk, listen to the birds, feel the gentle breeze, and thank Him, knowing He is mine as I am His. Life—with all its arduous details and never-ending to-do lists—is good.

On His Toes –
Life in Hollywood in the Early Days
Originally published on The Writings of A. K. Frailey 5/8/2012

Recently I discovered that my grandfather had written a book and that it was still available on Amazon, so I went ahead and I ordered it. After previewing a few pages, I went ahead and read it to the family. What an amazing joy it has been! It is a great story entitled *On His Toes* written by Irving T. McDonald (who was my mother's father), and it is all about a young man who goes to work for one of the first movie production companies of his day.

When I realized that this book was published by Dodd, Mead, and Company in 1921, it hit me that this was a first of its kind. The description of the production studios, the property rooms and all the things they used, the demanding but skilled abilities of the director and the actors, the plot involving this young guy trying to figure out what he wants to do with his life and his falling in love with the movie-making business, it sure makes for a great read.

I always knew that my grandfather was a talented man. He was a radio broadcaster for many years, and he worked in various teaching positions throughout his life, but surprisingly, I knew little about him personally. Reading this book has really helped me to get to know the man behind the name a bit better.

I suppose it is an all too familiar reality nowadays that we don't really know the very people who made our lives possible. I recently read my grandmother's memoirs (which is where I learned about my grandfather's book), and I discovered that Grandfather almost died during a flu epidemic, but for the kindness of a landlady and the generosity of a doctor, he would have died. My grandfather later married and had six children, one of whom was my mother. She grew up and married and had six children, one of whom was me, and I am now the mother of eight children. None of us would exist but for the kindness of those two strangers and my grandfather's strength of spirit, which enabled him to overcome the dangers of his environment and situation.

As I live and work in my little world, I think about all the people who have made my life possible, and I wonder about their lives and how our lives are intertwined even though we may never meet. I wonder about the people who made the car I am driving in, who designed it, and who sold it to us. I wonder about the people who made the roads I drive across and what their lives must have been like as they toiled away on hot summer days bridging rivers and forging through rock across our part of the nation. I wonder about the doctor who brought me into the world, and I wonder about all my relatives who have passed away, giving me the opportunity to live, to share their home, on earth. I carry their genes in my body, they are the blood of my blood, yet I know little more than their names.

Yet, as I read my grandfather's book, I came to realize that those who have gone before are not really gone, they are just someplace not within my present sight. And then I realize that I am the forerunner of all those who will come after me, and I feel amazed at the thought. I am only granted a small portion of time before I too must move on. And I wonder who will remember me, and I wonder what they will wonder about...

The Stuff of Life
Originally published on The Writings of A. K. Frailey 5/31/2012

I am not a shopper. I am not a hoarder. I do not enjoy having a lot of stuff. Thus, I sometimes get annoyed with a society that loves to get, collect, and pass along massive amounts of stuff. To me, a clear environment is akin to a clear mind. When I am busy taking care of "stuff," I tend to miss out on doing other things—things that I would much rather be doing.

As an example, my youngest daughter came to me recently and asked if she could go out and "meet the rain". I had a sudden flashback to when I was a young girl and went out to meet the rain myself. I remember having a glorious time just standing outside, watching and feeling the rain come down, and being amazed at the power and glory of nature. I so enjoyed the raw and primitive reality of a quiet, pattering rain. When my daughter came back inside a few minutes later, she was laughing, and she told me that she had gone into the "deepest, deepest rain." I knew exactly what she meant, and I was so happy for her.

Stuff is just stuff; it will not last. Stuff has a purpose in that we need stuff to eat, to wear, to live in, and the tools of our trade, but still, stuff can become a noose around our necks when we offer up the very purpose of our existence to the maintenance of all of our stuff—stuff that distracts us from God, from experiencing life and other people. Living simply with less stuff takes self-control, and it can be hard to get rid of stuff we have become attached to, but we make choices all the time, and choices involve a spirit of letting go. Our lives are a process of letting go, realizing that people we love will go on ahead without us, and we will have to leave others behind someday.

When my last day comes, I do not want to be filled with thoughts about the stuff of life but rather the relationships I have nourished and the life to come. I do not want to be filled with regrets of wasted time and opportunities. My days pass all too swiftly, and I want them filled with more than stuff.

Rather Like Poetry
Originally published on The Writings of A. K. Frailey 6/22/2012

I have met a few people in my life whose wisdom, though quiet and unpretending, has had a great influence on me. Most often, I do not know much of their history, but I always wonder—what made them so wise? When I've looked into it, I have come across a commonality: they all had to endure some seriously trying times. Often, they had to face their own limitations, tremendous frustrations, and even battles against temptation and evil.

One of the dearest and most decent of men I ever met was a Chinese professor who was living at our house while he was studying at the university. My mother rented rooms to foreign students, which was something of an education for me. This gentleman was so soft-spoken that when he did speak everyone listened, for he had a way of saying things that were incredibly beautiful—rather like poetry—very sincere and heartfelt. He noticed things, and he appreciated every detail of life.

I saw him as a strong and capable person, so I was not overly concerned when I knew it was time for him to return to China. But one afternoon, as we were enjoying a cup of tea at the kitchen table, he looked at me intently and told me that I needed to listen to him for a few minutes; he then proceeded to tell me about his life. He had been a successful professor, but one day, he gave a talk that praised democracy and shortly after that, he was taken from his home, away from his wife and child and parents, and he was made to work on a farm of some kind. It had been years since he had seen his family.

But with changing times, the government had decided to educate its people again, and he was called out from his servitude and sent to a university in America so that he could be a professor again, teaching what they wanted him to teach. I asked him why he didn't just stay in the U.S., but he said that he wanted to see his family again. He could not run away. It was better to be brave and face what he must face in China.

I asked him why he told me all this when there was nothing I could do to help; I was just a teenager at the time, and he said that he just wanted someone to know. And I have known and remembered his story all my life. I have prayed for him and his family. There are many people who have endured so much suffering, so much trial, so much grief, and yet they can still see goodness; they still believe in being brave, they can still experience lives of poetry....and mean it.

Sometimes, the greatest voices in the world are the quiet ones, the ones who have seen much, have experienced incredible things, though they will not say much about themselves. Yet, on a blessed day, we might have a conversation over a cup of tea, and our lives will be enriched and renewed forever.

Homeschooling
Originally published on The Writings of A. K. Frailey 7/31/2012

I teach a wide age range and enjoy the challenge. The fun part is seeing how far each child can reach mentally and spiritually while maintaining connections to their siblings. Some people wonder why I go to all the painstaking work of homeschooling when I could more easily put my kids into a public or private school. Though the answer is involved, I can simply state that homeschooling binds us together as a family like nothing else could. We learn together, we deal with problems together, we have fun together, we help each other, and we grow together.

My older kids enjoy giving the younger kids humorous previews of *what is coming next...* while the younger ones have a uniquely adapted educational experience. We have become self-starters and independent learners. Everyone *owns* their own curriculum. We go over books and material options together before I buy what we need, and as some zoom ahead in certain areas others choose to do more in-depth studies on a favorite subject. I realized long ago that it is best to have the kids involved early on in some of the educational planning because then they take responsibility for their education. Though they may not love a particular subject (spelling) they know they also have subjects (history) that they really do love. When motivation is embedded in the very learning process itself – so much the better.

We can't run away from problems. My kids and I have to face discipline issues right away, or disruptions will plague us all day. It is funny how the older kids hold the younger kids accountable for their attitudes and say things like: "That pout won't help you learn, and if you don't get over it, you might get stuck like that." Then they go on and tell a long ridiculous story about the second cousin of someone who actually did grimace all day and—you get the idea.

So as the school year gears up for another semester, I won't have as much time for writing and gardening and long rambling walks with the kids, but such is life. I have the duty and joy to raise each of my kids to rise to their potential. I want them to be great citizens of this world and the world to come. May God will give me the strength and wisdom to do so.

J. R. R. Tolkien
Originally published on The Writings of A. K. Frailey 8/9/2012

In my mind, J. R. R. Tolkien is a heroic figure. He understood that the greatness of humanity lies within each of us through our faithfulness to our daily mission. He was a Catholic, the son of a Catholic convert, and an ardent believer in God. It was under his influence that C.S. Lewis embraced the reality of Christianity. While a young man, he formed a club with some close friends, and despite the small size of the group, they had some very big aspirations. They believed that they had a mission to change the world, to make it a better place. As for many people during World War I (and later World War II), this vision was put to test when several of Tolkien's friends died. They were not able to live out their noble aspirations. But in a letter, Tolkien was reminded of their ardent dreams, and he was encouraged to go forward—to fulfill his own potential. He did. An ordinary man in so many ways, yet his faithfulness to his family, to his wife and children, his students, his friends, and his stories reach us today.

After I had read most of his major works and became astonished at his incredible insight and clarity, I decided to read more about him so I could better understand his background and his mindset. In one book (*J.R.R. Tolkien: A Biography* by Humphrey Carpenter), I read about one of his typical days, where his bicycle broke down, and he was late for dinner while a stack of papers waited at home to be corrected. I was nearly pulling my hair out thinking about the fact that he *could* have been home writing great literature. But then (after I became more reasonable), I realized it was because he knew how to fix a bicycle, cared about being home for dinner, made it to meetings, and corrected innumerable papers that he was the kind of man who could write so faithfully about the human heart and the reality of suffering as well as the idiosyncratic silliness of common human interactions.

Tolkien, like many of his characters, could not predict the future, but he was engaged in humanity's struggle to overcome evil nevertheless. May I today aspire to the same noble faithfulness of a simple Hobbit—and an honest writer.

Angels
Originally published on The Writings of A. K. Frailey 9/26/2012

One of the happiest moments of my life was when I first discovered the *Catechism of the Catholic Church*. In that source, I found the core truths of my faith written out in clear, easy-to-understand language. One of my first big surprises—strange to say—was to affirm that angels are real.

That opened doors for me spiritually speaking because it broadened my field of vision. You might say I came to glimpse the greater world of God's supernatural existence. And this revelation has been comforting and startling in more ways than I can explain. But for starters, I'll go back to the source and share with you some of the things I learned that widened the universe for me.

"The existence of the spiritual, non-corporeal beings that Sacred Scripture usually calls 'angels' is a truth of faith. St. Augustine says: 'Angels' is the name of their office, not of their nature. If you seek the name of their nature, it is 'spirit'; if you seek the name of their office, it is 'angel': from what they are, 'spirit', from what they do, 'angel.' With their whole beings, the angels are servants and messengers of God.....they are the 'mighty ones who do his word, hearkening to the voice of the word.' As purely spiritual creatures, angels have intelligence and will: they are personal and immortal creatures, surpassing in perfection all visible creatures, as the splendor of their glory bears witness." – Catechism of the Catholic Church (paragraphs 328-329)

Sometimes, when the troubles of this world seem too much to bear—it helps to know that we are not alone. God made angels who go before us and alongside us and help us along our way.

Music
Originally published on The Writings of A. K. Frailey 5/14/2014

There are a lot of sounds in the world, but it tends to be the simple ones that move my heart the most. I love to hear the sound of a single bird announcing the day and the way a chorus of chirping voices grows to an orchestra of gladness. I love to hear the laughter of children as they play and the tune a person resonates when his or her spirit is happy.

Our kids started piano lessons young, and one has chosen to move from the piano to the violin. Music lessons are an investment in money, time, energy, and patience, but as I listen to them play each day, I realize I have received much more than I ever gave. They play classical music, themes from movies, hymns ancient and new, patriotic marches, and music I never heard before but which moves my soul nonetheless.

Like any real art, music is a source of grace. It is a reflection of God's astounding beauty, and it cannot be contained. Once you make music, you enrich the very air around you, and you can change the world. Even when I am most irritated, angry, disappointed, frightened or despairing, when I hear the kids playing music, my soul is lifted, and my spirit is recharged.

So, as I thank God for all His glory, I am grateful for all the sounds that make our world a better place and our children's amazing ability to play musical instruments.

Through their passion, the world is born anew.

Mortal Eyes
Originally published on The Writings of A. K. Frailey 5/20/2014

There's life...and then there's life.

When I read a good book, I feel like I get the value, meaning, purpose, and passion of life's struggles better than when I am just doing the ordinary duties of the day. The kids and I are currently reading *Anne of Green Gables,* a story where the author draws out the fantastic elements of the ordinary. Her descriptions of a sunrise and sunset allow me to see the grandeur of the moment. I see through her eyes more powerfully than my own. When reading a *What if...* story like *Flowers for Algernon,* I understand the value of a human soul a little better. Strange?

Perhaps it is because writers try to see what is lost in the glare of "ordinary." They try to recover what we forget to notice. We all have the potential to be a good writer, if not to put things down on paper, at least to look again and see what is before us with new and vivid appreciation.

Well-trained actors do much the same. They take real life, act it out, play it up, and help us to see what is right in front of us. Authentic writers and actors can help the blind see and the deaf hear. Life is meant to be lived passionately, but it takes skill and determination to do that. Occasionally, we can be pulled from the ordinary into the extraordinary and reminded that there is more to us than we see with our mortal eyes.

Home Management

Originally published on The Writings of A. K. Frailey 6/4/2014

Warning—if someday you happen to be walking along and you cross in front of one of your otherwise innocent-looking appliances and just happen to notice a bit of something (could be dirt, could be a crayon, could be one of last year's pasta dinner experiments) sticking out from underneath and you hear a little voice saying: "Maybe I should just check…." Stop! This could lead you places you *do not* want to go. Trust me.

I just spent the morning facing things that I really didn't want to know existed. There are more dirt and goo under appliances than are dreamt of in Man's philosophy, Horatio!

The worst part is that even if you do happen to come out of the whole experience victorious, and you stand up again (dirtier but still a semblance of your former self), sure, there you are—facing a house full of *other appliances* looking at you…and now you know what they are hiding.

Listen—while there is still time—Home Management isn't everything it's cracked up to be. Ignore that dust ball, kick the crayon further back, go outside, play ball with your kids, and refresh your spirit with something wholesome. Dirt exists, it is a part of life…and frankly…appliances LIKE to collect things. Let them have their little fun.

May the best housekeeper learn her limits.

A Deeply Disturbed Ocean
Originally published on The Writings of A. K. Frailey 9/3/2014

Occasionally there are electric moments while reading the words of another person when you realize that though that person may have lived years before, you share something—a deep abiding interest, a concern, an insight, a hope, or a fear.

So, I discovered such a moment recently while reading about the life of Winston Churchill. He was a man who appeared to have failed, much like his father before him, but in the end, he triumphed, and he brought the world with him in that triumph. His words before that triumph planted the seeds of his future success. It was in his heart and soul to believe that right was right, truth existed, and that we must not lose our way in this world. Here are some of his words that struck me forcibly this week. They echo loudly into our world today.

"We are a race doubtful of its mission and no longer confident about its principles, infirm of purpose, drifting to and fro with the tides and currents of a deeply disturbed ocean. The compass has been damaged. The charts are out of date. The crew have to take it in turns to be Captain, and every captain before every movement of the helm has to take a ballot not only of the crew but of an ever-increasing number of passengers..." (Mr. Churchill by Philip Guedalla p.242)

"Laws, just or unjust, may govern men's actions. Tyrannies may restrain or regulate their words. The machinery of propaganda may pack their minds with falsehoods. But the soul of man thus held in trance or frozen in a long night can be awakened by a spark coming

from God knows where. People in bondage need not despair." (Churchill in Memoriam New York Times p.154)

In our times—trying as they may be—let us remember that we never walk alone. The question for us to ponder has never been—Is God with me? But rather—Am I with God?
We shall be known by our fruit.

A World Worth Saving
Originally published on The Writings of A. K. Frailey 9/8/2014

Recently, I read that there have been several cases where surrogate mothers discovered that they were carrying babies with Down syndrome, and they were told to abort their babies by the biological parents, but they refused and decided to keep the babies.

I have also read that Richard Dawkins believes that it is immoral to allow a "Down Syndrome baby" to come to term. Notice, for him, the *syndrome* comes first, not the humanity of the baby. For him, abortion is the only moral option. I have to wonder at this current attitude in the face of the barbaric cruelty of ISIS. After all, they believe that killing infidels is the only moral option. Sometimes, those infidels are little children.

The other day, as I was walking with my son in the late evening, mourning over the recent gruesome tragedies inflicted by ISIS, my son asked me how come it was gruesome for ISIS to behead men, women, and children, but there was little moral outrage when babies in the womb were dismembered and beheaded. Abortion is every bit as violent as ISIS, but it is funded by US tax dollars. Millions of babies have been brutally murdered through abortion in the last thirty years. It is so horrifically common it seems to slip by people's conscious thought. Every day in the US, we basically behead innocent babies.

This leads me back to the eugenics movement to rid the world of people with Down Syndrome. I find it interesting that Christians and Down Syndrome children are especially targeted for extermination. Why is that? The people I have known with Down Syndrome, and the parents who care for them, tend to be happy people. In fact, one mother I know who recently lost her adult daughter with Down Syndrome to cancer told me that her daughter was the best gift she ever had. Her daughter taught her to love in a way she had never experienced before.

Clearly, people with Down Syndrome are still people. Just as Christians are still people, even though they may not believe what ISIS believes. Yet in both cases, there are those who would convince the world that we all would be better off without them. Their kind. Their influence. What is the danger exactly? Are they hurting anyone? Are they aggressively trying to take over the world?

No, they just ask something of us that perhaps we do not want to give. People with Down Syndrome ask for an unconditional love, which they, more often than not, fully return. Christians ask for a sacrificial love, which, when lived as Christ lived, is also fully returned.

I have to ask myself – what are we saving the world from? Love? Perhaps we need to wonder less if we are *saving the world,* but rather, are we making a *world worth saving?*

What Makes Heroes So Heroic?
Originally published on The Writings of A. K. Frailey 10/10/2014

All heroes struggle, but it is their very struggle to overcome their weaker selves that their true heroism is born.

Heroes believe in something beyond themselves, and their belief leads to conviction, and conviction draws them into action.

Heroes keep faith with faith.

Heroes are capable of deep, enduring love.

Heroes offer and receive spiritual gifts.

Heroes pay a price for their choices.

Tolkien loved and wrote about heroes. In the process—he became one.

Eight Kids and Grateful
Originally published on The Writings of A. K. Frailey 1/21/2015

The other day I was speaking to a woman on the phone who, for practical reasons, needed to know a little more about me and my family. When she discovered that I had eight children and, worse yet, that my husband died when they were all under 18, I thought she would have a stroke. She left little doubt in my mind that I must be crazy.

I'm not sure what exactly she thought I should do—renumber my kids or simply never mention them, but her tone suggested I had made an indelicate mistake in even admitting I had eight children—under any circumstances.

In some kind of perverse reaction, rather than crumbling into a heap of repentant grief, I further distanced myself from decent society by proclaiming that I also homeschool my kids, and I really enjoy being around them.

Her response was, "Whatever!"

I was clearly beyond all hope.

Did I fall upon my knees in prayer for the poor woman's soul? No. Good idea—it just never occurred to me. She would undoubtedly be baffled by my pity, so I'll call it compassion, but honestly, it would be pity. I pity anyone who sincerely believes that children are little more than burdens, or that no one could seriously want and welcome eight kids—especially under trying circumstances.

When my husband was diagnosed with Leukemia, my youngest was only seven months old. Besides the terrible grief I felt for my suffering husband was the realization that we would never know the joy of welcoming another baby into the world. As it is, the eight children I've been blessed with have shared their strength, their candor, their honesty, their love, their hard work, their sense of honor, and their noble spirits with me and many others.

The other day, as I stared at two large feed sacks, I knew I could not lift, my eldest son stepped over without a word, and swooped them into his arms and put them where they belonged. God knew what He was doing when He gave me son #1. And #2, who has a sense of humor that lightens the mood even in the hardest moments. And #3, who is a world-class student, manages the chicken establishment on our place and mops floors on the side. #4 is the family cook and storyteller, #5 is our artist par-excellence, #6 helps me organize, #7 helps keep the critters happy, and #8 keeps us laughing.

There will always be people who think I'm crazy for having eight kids.

Whatever!

I couldn't be more grateful.

Lenten Faith
Originally published on The Writings of A. K. Frailey 2/18/2015

"Faith is the daring of the soul to go farther than it can see." ~William Newton Clark

"I believe in the sun even when it isn't shining. I believe in love even when I am alone. I believe in God even when He is silent." ~ WW II refugee

Lent has just begun. For some, this time of the year is business as usual. For some, it is an intense time of prayer and sacrifice. For me, it is both.

Each season has its own challenges and rewards. This holy season, which the Church wisely treats with grave respect, is an opportunity to remember the end point of my existence—to take some time to reflect on why I am here at this time, sharing the world with this particular generation. The sacrifices of meat and meals, of small hardships, accepted without obvious irritation, the offerings of kindness and goodwill, help me to practice the heroic aspects of my best self in preparation for my final end when everything will be made clear.

Do you remember Sunday nights as a kid when you realized that Monday was coming and that nothing you did or said could change that reality? The weekend was over. School was coming. For me, it was like a mini-death. As I remember, I was rather specific about my regrets. I think about that as I ponder the end of my earthly journey. I doubt I'll be moaning that I wish I had eaten more, played more games, been a bit more selfish, or slept in more often.

My faith informs me that God exists, and He created me for a noble purpose. Lent is a time, despite all the hurry and bustle of over-filled days, to ponder how I am spending my life and what I might regret. In the final analysis, anything that draws me closer to God is a blessing, even if it is painful. Lenten faith does indeed dare the soul to go farther than it can see.

You Converted Him—Right?
Originally published on The Writings of A. K. Frailey 3/4/2015

Recently I was explaining to a new friend that my father is an agnostic historian, who specialized in canon law, while my brother is a Catholic, a canon lawyer-priest. I got a disconcerting reaction. "Well, you converted him (meaning my dad, I presume), right?"

Gee, not yet.

I have a wide variety of people in my life—and some would rather not think about God. The words "God bless" at the end of a conversation seem to send shivers down their spines. Does that mean I should disown them? Or, better yet, get busy and convert them?

Conversion isn't in my power. Love is, though. And love is amazingly effective at putting people in the right mood for a conversion experience. Though I live some distance from my dad, we manage to have weekly conversations that ramble through our lives and into our hearts. My dad may say he doesn't give God much of a chance of existing, but I do. And in his connection to me, he can't help but be connected to God. I've prayed, I've offered sacrifices, and I've come within millimeters of giving up, but I always remember that here, in this unexplored, un-faithful zone, lies the mercy of God. He gets to decide what will happen with my dad on the long road. My job is to love him while I have the chance.

There are so many people who have lost touch with God and thus lost the touch of God. Their hearts have hardened, and they believe that they do not need Him. They can be good without Him. They love and live as deeply as anyone. Someday, they may come to understand that it was God, inside them all along, that made their loves and lives possible. But until then, I can only hope, stay close, and keep on loving them. After all, it's what God has been doing all along.

Untutored Wisdom
Originally published on The Writings of A. K. Frailey 4/8/2015

Children see the world differently. Well, from me anyway. With my *vast* years of experience, I tend to observe critically and reach conclusions based on my carefully *cultured* wisdom. Children tend to just *see,* and since they don't have as many filters, they tend to report what they see with some accuracy. Their untutored wisdom often leaves me humbled, baffled, intrigued, at times laughing out loud, and certainly, never quite the same.

The other day, as my sons were going out on a mission of mercy to help their grandparents with some heavy lifting jobs, I passed the keys to one son and wished him well. My six-year-old offered this insight instead: *"If the blue car doesn't work, try the gray one, and if that doesn't work, ask for help, and if that doesn't work—walk."* Who knew someone so little could consider the options so honestly?

One springtime, my little son looked outside and saw new buds greening up the trees. He came running up to me, saying: *"Look, Mom, God's dressing up the trees for Easter."* Yes, of course, He was—I'd just never grasped that so clearly before.

And one year, as a play-dead possum lay in the yard after my husband had tried rather unsuccessfully to shoo it away, one daughter carefully observed: *"Well, you can't chase a dead possum."* Too true. Apparently, Mr. Opossum was in on that bit of insight.

Through the years of raising my kids, I often had the experience of stopping everything just to think about what I just heard coming out of their little/big mouths, minds, and hearts. And it is not just the little ones who have rearranged my thinking—teenagers are quite proficient at tossing my preconceived notions to the wind. Yet my soul has been enriched beyond measure by their words, by their wisdom, by their honest insight.

Sometimes the greatest treasure we can bestow on the world is to actually hear—even when we think we're listening.

Gardening Grace
Originally published on The Writings of A. K. Frailey 4/15/2015

Gardens are like family: they demand attention; they can get out of hand really quick, yet they feed you in ways nothing else can. For all of my aches and pains, my dislike of getting muddy, and my squeamish attitude about bugs that live in colonies, I am willing, year after year, to start the garden over again. This year is no exception. Considering the work involved and the many family needs demanding my attention, I had to think long and hard about this particular vocation before I even got started. Is gardening really worth my time and effort? After all, I could buy almost everything I want at the grocery store. But in the end, I was converted toward the wholesome reality of a family garden by a few simple but profound truths.

#1 **A garden draws me into the natural world far from technology.**
With all of society's advancements—it is good to get away from the computer screen and worldly concerns and reacquaint myself with the good earth. Plants and animals have been here a lot longer than our human-made tools and toys, and they still have something to say to me—if I dare to listen.

#2 **Gardens demand a lot and give a lot.**
They require consistent effort. They force a person into a serious commitment of time, sweat, and occasional tears. If I don't take care, weeds take over. If I don't protect it, the garden will die. This simple reality reminds me of a basic truth in every important relationship: no love, no stewardship—no fruit.

#3 **I know what goes into my garden, so I know what goes into me.**
This may seem paranoid but in a world of pesticides, herbicides, antibiotics for animals, and various other unknowns, I like to know what feeds the animals and plants which feed me. Cancer has struck too close to home to assume that every chemical remedy is a good one.

#4 **There is a correlation to God as Creator and myself as a gardener.**
When I plant a seed, I know it is His seed, I know He forms and shapes the life that comes from the seed, and I know that all the growing universe is His—but in my small world, I can cultivate a small part of it, making it orderly, beautiful and fruitful. When faced with international disasters, national worries, and personal struggles, it is no small comfort to enjoy God's life in a garden—gardening grace—I call it. And so it is.

#5 **My final reason is purely mercenary.**
I enjoy knowing that I have stocked some food away for a rainy, stormy, or snowy day. I never know what the future will bring. Having a few jars of homemade jam, pickles, or salsa, some onions & herbs hanging in the kitchen, some frozen peppers, corn, squash, and pumpkin stocked in the freezer, makes my life a little more comfortable. Despite my aching back, my heart is at ease knowing my garden is there, waiting for me in the morning.

Interior Life
Originally published on The Writings of A. K. Frailey 6/24/2015

"The soul that begins to have interior life appreciates the treasure it bears within its heart. Each day it will make a greater effort to deny admission into the mind of an image that prevents or hinders the soul's close contact with God." (*In Conversation with God* p. 313 paragraph 3)

The whole concept of an interior life intrigues me. I've read about saints with highly developed interior lives, and I often find myself longing to be so holy, but as my life catapults through each day, I can't help but realize that my eight children, my garden, my bit of writing, are all doorways to the interior world of God's life. I need not be jealous—I just need courage.

Someone once said, "Hell is other people." Could it not be true that Heaven is other people also? I glimpse the eternity of a soul when I look into another person's eyes. As it is quite apparent that God put us here on Earth, together, for a purpose—I contemplate the possibilities. Perhaps in the act of opening ourselves to the larger reality of other people's vision, struggles, hopes, and crushing failures, we come to see not just the ideal that God has for us, but the grief of the cross lived through broken dreams and the ennobled daring to rise again.

In today's world, I suppose in every generation, we are faced with a multitude of "hells"— human beings' failure to love as He loves. But we are also given a daily opportunity to escape hell by overcoming the hate which feels so natural to us. Hate is no cure. It offers no hope or redemptive recovery. Its cousin, bitterness, is only a shadow leading to further darkness of spirit.

It is in the cultivation of an interior life that I allow the grace of God to strengthen me to overcome all the negative influences in my life and open myself to the possible joys of life and hope of things yet to come. Some would say I am using a crutch to help me over the hard parts. All I know is that through an interior life, I find my life. And through the eyes of others, I glimpse the possibility of Hell—or Heaven.

Simple Summer

Originally published on The Writings of A. K. Frailey 7/8/2015

I'm sitting outside on the back porch, while Merry, the cat—a poor injured stray we saved—is sitting at my feet doing what cats do…resting and checking out the world whenever the mood hits. The pine trees sway in a gentle breeze while white, fluffy clouds sail serenely overhead. We've had a lot of rain lately, so everything is green and gorgeous. A red rose in a nearby pot practically glows against the backdrop of pine trees. Various summer flowers bloom in their summertime brilliance. Flies and bees and a little jumping spider have also made an appearance. The chicks, still in the brooder house waiting for their outdoor pen, are running about, trying their wings as they learn that the ground cannot hold them bound.

The awesome beauty of this summer day, the chirping multitude: sparrows, red-wing blackbirds, robins, cardinals, and cooing doves, the laughter of young children at play, the haunting melody played by one of the girls at the piano, rustling waves of breezes cascading over the fields of corn and beans all work together, creating a pallet of beauty that any artist would envy.

When I considered what to write on my blog today, no words would come. Yet as I sit here surrounded by simple summer, I find I do not need words—just eyes and ears and a heart willing to believe that this is real.

When the winter winds blow, the sky laden with gray clouds, and the birds silenced in their nests, I will remember this day. The yellow buttercups, the red rose, the buzzing bees will live in my heart and imagination. Even in my dreams, I will remember this day, and no matter the clouds or the cold and the barren waste of winter, summer will yet live.

Acceptance
Originally published on The Writings of A. K. Frailey 7/15/2015

Yesterday, I took two of my kids to the oral surgeon to get their wisdom teeth removed. The trip down was okay, the trip back, very quiet. As I drove through the last of a rainstorm which had moved through that morning, adjusting for all the construction barriers and trying to hold back useless questions, like: "Are you feeling all right?" I pondered the question of suffering—once again.

I remember the surprising answer my priest offered me after a miscarriage. Instead of telling me what to do to alleviate my suffering or how to get around the pain, his first recommendation was to "accept what you cannot change." Not exactly what I wanted to hear. In time, I learned the wisdom of his words.

We suffer for a lot of reasons, sometimes at the hands of others, sometimes through our own fault, and sometimes, like wisdom teeth, for no apparent reason at all. Simply recognizing the pain we are in is the first step to dealing with it effectively.

In my kids' case, they knew that oral surgery would hurt, but they also knew that impacted wisdom teeth would cause worse suffering later if they didn't deal with it now. I knew that taking my kids to an oral surgeon would involve pain, but it was a price I was willing to pay to save them more grief later. There are a lot of times when we are forced to realize that suffering is inevitable and asking why or being angry is useless, actually hindering the healing process. The human body is packed full of opportunities to suffer. But that fact need not leave us hopeless. When we accept that suffering exists, that it in itself is not evil, then we can learn the value of acceptance.

A friend, a mother of two teens diagnosed with cancer, told me after she had been informed that she had only weeks to live, that "It is what it is." In most people, I would have thought this reaction one of despair or mere resignation, but after walking the road of faith through all the stages of death with Carla, I realized how complete she had become. She accepted the presence of death. She did everything she could to say her grateful goodbyes and to leave in the most loving manner possible, and she died at peace.

When my kids suffered from swollen, aching jaws, I handed them their medication, gave them the directions, and reminded them to be careful. (I also handed them containers of ice cream and strawberry yogurt.) My teens have a choice—deal with what is honestly, realizing that pain will be a part of their healing, or make things worse by trying to avoid it.

This morning, as I said my prayers, I remembered the cross of Christ, and though I knew I would have to face this day's allotment of suffering, I also knew through the love that Christ bears us, that suffering need not be wasted. It is also an opportunity to love and be loved—if we accept it.

A Change of Perspective
Originally published on The Writings of A. K. Frailey 9/2/2015

Today's Gospel reading was the parable of the talents and the sin of omission, so when the boys brought in buckets *and buckets* of apples this morning, I could hardly ignore them. It would have been a sin to waste so much good fruit, even if they aren't the prettiest apples in the world. They are the ones that grow on *my* trees, the gifts that God has given us this year, and though I had a long to-do list, I shoved everything aside to work on those apples.

I found myself working alone at first, but as I assigned jobs and the kids found their peelers and slicers and sat down to work, they also found their humor. It was not long before an "I-don't-have-time-for-this" silence was replaced with, "Remember when we…"

Since I was the senior cook in charge of the canning, I had to make sure the apples were spiced with sugar and cinnamon before going into the hot jars and then into the even hotter boiling bath. In the midst of all this, a water filter had to be changed and a couple band-aids applied, but I found myself listening to the kids reminiscing about other family activities, some of which I had never known about… And I realized that life really is what happens when you are planning other things. It is in accomplishing the jobs at hand that creates the warmest memories.

When we first moved out here nearly twenty years ago, I used to listen to the farmers' wives talk about the 20 quarts of jam they put up or the 40 pints they froze. At the time, I was rather underwhelmed by their accomplishments simply because I was so blatantly ignorant of how much work it took to put up a measly seven jars of anything. Now I know better. I also understand why they smiled when they reminisced. They weren't just proud of their accomplishments; they had enjoyed the time with family, the stories swapped, the jokes played on each other. I can envision what it was like because we have repeated the process several times now.

Perhaps, at first, it does seem like just another big job, and I have to hand out paring knives like a drill sergeant, but after a bit, those talents which seemed like a burden, quickly repay the effort. The kids and I have a change of perspective and perhaps a change of heart, too. Life is in the little moments.

When a Leaf Falls
Originally published on The Writings of A. K. Frailey 10/28/2015

As I look out the window watching the autumn leaves swirl to the ground, I can't help thinking about my brother's death last week. There is a parable of sorts in every bit of nature; the autumn leaves are no exception. I find nature's lessons to be healing in a sad and troubled world.

The first thing that strikes me is that when all is calm, the leaves appear to fall one by one. You can sit by and appreciate their particular glory as they fall. Yet, when the wind blows harshly, the swirl becomes overwhelming and you lose the individuality of each as they become part of a massive array of color and texture so strong that it takes on a power all its own.

Hence the reality of the refugees who are suffering and dying as a group, as mere numbers in a tragic statistic. My brother could have been regulated to a statistic, but for those who knew and cared about him, he was much more than that. Though my family is imperfect, our efforts to do right by him remain nonetheless. His life was personal, his death was personal, and he is more than another sad statistic.

There are times for statistics. There are times to analyze the big picture. A large-scale framework allows us to take a proper assessment of what is happening and take proper action. But if all we offer is large-scale solutions, clean-up services for the yard, relief services for the poor, money allotted to causes, we forget that there are unique and poignant stories in every life and death. There are, at this moment, hearts in grief, aged people suffering from loneliness, frightened children, and hungry families.

When a leaf falls, it is a bittersweet beauty because, though it is an end, it is also a beginning. Spring growth will rise from the death of the leaf. But when a heart falls, when a person's soul despairs, there is no new growth. There is only death. That is the greatest tragedy that can happen in this adventure we call life.

Yet, there are solutions to our problems. Lots of solutions. If only we are willing to engage. Projects and plans for the poor, political solutions for the refugee crises, money for the needy, are all valid and helpful. But above all, we must never forget the beauty of the individual life.

There is no one so isolated from the rest of humanity that he or she can't find someone to care about. In caring, so we find our beauty and when it is our turn to fall, we'll find ourselves more than a statistic in the hearts of others who will discover in us the strength of new hope.

Love Is Life
Originally published on The Writings of A. K. Frailey 11/4/2015

I graduated from college a long time ago. But I've never stopped learning. In fact, as I served in various schools and in the Peace Corps and eventually became a home-schooling mother, I have encountered a multitude of new, rather steep, learning curves. Presently, I am learning at a faster rate than ever before.

This past year I learned how to help my son navigate through the difficulties of a long-distance, online college education, and I am presently considering the next three kids' futures. They are facing a vastly different world than the one I grew up in. Technology is huge and understanding its place in the world is necessary to succeed in pretty much every field. College tuitions are so high now that for one child, I could easily spend more than I did to buy my house. The consequences of accepting loans are considerable. Choices have strings attached and learning everything I can about higher-education options is vitally important for my family's health.

I have also been learning how to handle the many house and property issues which creep up on a daily basis. I've learned to ask for help and hire experts who can solve issues like broken stoves and stuck drainage pipes, but I've also learned that there are things which I can do to avoid problems before they arise. The old adage, "A stitch in time...." is very true! It helps to know where the well-pump turn-off value is too.

There was a time when the mere thought of handling large gatherings at meals, organizing classes day-in-and-day-out, and maintaining a bustling home would have sent me into a panic. But panic really isn't an option. In every home, the hardest part is being involved in the daily lives of those around you. I should say, being aware of the spiritual welfare of those around you. The "stitch in time" adage applies. As human beings, we go through an incredible amount of change and stress in the course of a day, a week, a month and a lifetime. What happened yesterday may still color our mood tomorrow. In today's technological information-overloaded society, this is especially true. Our kids are immersed in a turbulent sea of information and disinformation. Recognizing mood swings, depression, creeping irritation, a deep-seated sadness, over-arching pride, or a whole host of other emotional and spiritual dangers is vastly important for the success of a family. And deciding which action to take involves another field of expertise. Not something one learns in a day...it takes a lifetime.

But in all these learning experiences, I have found one common ingredient: to care makes learning meaningful. Whether I am learning how to teach, how to fix a faucet, how to love, I know that the most vital aspect of life-long learning is the love with which we approach the situation, be it a lecture or a broken heart.

If I have learned anything, it is that love itself is life.

A Culture of Encounter
Originally published on The Writings of A. K. Frailey 11/18/2015

Sister Constance Veit wrote an article in the *Catholic Times* recently where she relates meeting Pope Francis when he showed up at the home of the Little Sisters of the Poor in Washington D.C. Her joyful experience reflects Pope Francis' lived message, calling us toward an "encounter culture" lifestyle. I love that expression, and I have thought about it a lot these past few days.

As I go about my daily duties, teaching, studying, cleaning, cooking, talking with the kids, I am reminded that every moment can be an "encounter moment." To be honest, my day often feels like a well-intentioned resolve that devolves into a series of colliding events: a day at the circus, but nobody gets paid.

But every so often, I catch myself in the midst of what might appear to be random chaos, and I stop and pray the moment from meaningless madness toward a purposeful encounter. I have prayed in an encounter moment while correcting papers, I have prayed in an encounter moment while standing outside under a perfect autumn sky, I have prayed in an encounter moment while chatting on the phone, while talking with one of my children, while making bread, while knitting... In fact, I have discovered that there is no moment that can't suddenly be lifted from the mundane to the momentous by a few seconds of reflected prayer. In those brief ticks of the clock, I become truly aware of the present value of the encounter before me, opening myself to all that grace has to offer. Long evening shadows falling against a wall, the smell of wood smoke curling up the chimney, the wispy tendrils of hair falling over my daughter's cheek, all become sources of wonder. I discover treasures hidden in plain sight.

I suspect this meaningful moment is the whole purpose of art, to remind us of these mysterious treasures, to have an "encounter" with our own lives. Pope Francis speaks to the whole world, reminding us of profound realities when he reminds us to live intentionally, to live as a culture of encounter. In truth, there is nothing too profound for the human heart, if we allow God's grace to enter and encounter Him in everything.

Encounter Culture
Originally published on The Writings of A. K. Frailey 12/9/2015

I am blatantly stealing the term *"Encounter Culture"* from Pope Francis—but I don't think he'll mind. I hope not...

As I consider the last days before Christmas begins, I think about the ways in which I miss the whole point of the season, year after swiftly passing year. I tend to get caught up in the details of shopping, sending out cards, finishing school assignments, getting cookies baked and decorated, remembering to take things out of the freezer to defrost... I get so tired that my soul lays down and begs for a rest.

So, I try to make up for my spiritual emptiness by praying in the evening. Unfortunately, my body thinks this is a good time to turn off my brain. And so it is. I am finding that praying is a sort of emptying experience. I have to stop and *not* be efficient for a bit. My to-do lists get shoved to the side and my self-esteem wilts as guilt kicks in, but then, I reevaluate my life.

Here is a little thought that has helped me remember the "reason for the season" and hug my relationship with God a little tighter:

If I miss God in my life, will I find Him at my death?

December 15th was the 2nd anniversary of my husband's death after a four-year battle with leukemia. My daughter and I went to his gravesite last weekend and placed flowers next to his tombstone—which bears my name as well. Charles Dickens was right on the mark when in *The Christmas Carol* he has old Scrooge finally relent and change his life when he sees his tombstone bearing his name. There is something relentless about confronting your name inscribed in stone and place your feet on the dead grass where your body will someday lie.

My heart beats at the command of God. I don't want to face a hole where a relationship with the Eternal should have been.

Each Christmas is a reminder of a universal truth—God lives, and He comes to us as both Man and God for our salvation.

I may not be able to tuck that under the tree, but my life can live the truth of it as I unwrap the gift of each day.

The Blessed
Originally published on The Writings of A. K. Frailey 1/23/2016

In this troubled world where it seems that there are very few heroes left, except the imaginary ones, it is nice to come across a real, beautifully valiant spirit.

I was reading The Knights of Columbus magazine *Columbia* and came across an article on the life of Blessed Laszlo. So I looked him up and discovered a hero. A man who, from an early age, felt drawn to helping the poor, who became a doctor and stayed true to his dream and assisted the poor even after inheriting a title, a castle, and all the good fortune of such an honor. He married, had a large family, and raised his children in the faith, teaching them the value of concrete acts of charity. This was a man who could have gloried in his good luck but rather gloried in God. He is remembered as "the doctor of the poor." Not a bad way to be remembered. I doubt God forgot his kindness.

There are heroes in our midst, but they may not be saving the world. They may be saving a life, someone's sanity, or mending a broken heart. They may be holding a limp hand, encouraging a discouraged heart, staying faithful to a vow, or working behind the scenes without notice. But in their honest endeavors, the heart of a valiant spirit beats in tune with God's mighty rhythm. Their work is not their own. Their lives reflect the best humanity has to offer the universe for the present and the future.

They are The Blessed.

Life in Lent
Originally published on The Writings of A. K. Frailey 2/6/2016

I have noticed a definite trend as I move through the homeschool week.

On Monday morning, I am speaking in active sentences packed with spelling words, circulating around the room, radiating energy and enthusiasm as I multi-task to my heart's content.

On Tuesday, I am still circulating, albeit a little slower; my sentences are a bit shorter, more to the point, there's a tad less spark to my demeanor.

On Wednesday, I'm still moving but rather jerkily; my sentences no longer bear any resemblance to the week's lessons. As a matter of fact, I am struggling to remember what language I speak.

By Thursday, I'm sitting in my chair as I ply through the texts, gesturing for the kids to come to me and explain what's happening in history, writing, science, math, and whatever else I dare to teach.

By Friday, a grunt, a gesture, a sticker, and we're good to go.

Well, it's not quite that bad... But the trend from energetic to slow motion is real enough. So is the brain-drain. I suspect that as coffee drinkers hooked on the whole concept of fast and effective, we tend to give ourselves little space to be anything but perfectly attuned to the nuances of constant multi-tasking. Yet, is that real? Are we real? What happens by the end of the week is reflected in what is happening inside of us as we attempt to be what we are not.

No one is perfect. No one can be "up" all the time. No one is beautiful every minute of the day. We get tired. We get exhausted. We get messy. To be honest, I think our whole nation is on the verge of a nervous breakdown. We try so hard to be up and energetic, beautiful and cool. Yet, we have been tucking our problems out of the way: debt, family breakdown, cultural divisions, spiritual emptiness.

Next week, Ash Wednesday kicks off the start of Lent. Some might think that this is simply another task to put on the to-do list. But, on the contrary, it is really a call to freedom. "Remember, man, from dust you came to dust you shall return." In our Lenten reflection, we actually become free to take a little "down time" to think about who we are and where we are going. We may not be effective and efficient for six weeks, but consider this as our "fast" for the duration. We can offer up our never-ending multi-tasking schedule and spend some time thinking about who we are and why we are alive. Life in Lent can be a soul-nurturing event.

Maybe by Easter, we'll feel reborn. After all, that's kind of the point...

Hero's Quest
Originally published on The Writings of A. K. Frailey 2/13/2016

In my never-ending quest for heroes, I am joyfully surprised when God keeps putting inspiring, life-changing stories in my path.

Here's another report from *Columbia* magazine, January 2016. It is the story of Kathleen Bravo, who, after experiencing some very dark days, entered a new phase of her life when she took over and rebranded a nonprofit organization, naming it Obria Medical Clinics. She has since touched the lives of many thousands of women and saved the lives of over six thousand babies. In the Columbia Magazine article, it states: "Our main goal is to meet a woman where she is – that is Mother Teresa's approach." And later, she says: "Don't limit the Holy Spirit." (p.8-9)

I love to absorb the stories of men and women who accept the risk of caring for our fellow human beings even when life is hard, the past has been disappointing, and the future looks questionable.

The question for us each day is not, "Do I have a choice?" since we always have a choice. The question is, what price are we willing to pay for our choices? Men and women who choose to fight for the good of others despite the challenges of misunderstanding and outright discrimination are real heroes.

My choice? I choose to focus on the best of humanity, what draws us together and makes us proud of our race. Who knows, but we may not be alone in this universe. How would another race view us?

If we don't value the most vulnerable among us…will anyone?

Real World Disconnect
Originally published on The Writings of A. K. Frailey 2/27/2016

Some people would say that we are more connected to the world than ever, but I wonder if this is really true. I heard a statistic this week that suicide is the third leading cause of death for teens. That tragic information made me pause. Why would teens, in a world full of options, choose to end their lives?

What are kids connected to? Or disconnected from? They are connected to the vast information web. They are connected to sound bites and superficial relationships built on Facebook and Twitter. They are connected to pictures, images, and sounds, but too often, they're disconnected to what is happening right in front of them.

What actually feeds us—spiritually and physically? I do not get fed by social media interactions. Even email has its limitations. That is not to say that these technological innovations don't have their purpose and value. But it is to ask, what are we crowding out when we engage in them to the exclusion of other forms of human communication and interaction?

When I took my kids to the lake yesterday, and they ran around watching the geese and ducks, sat and enjoyed the sun setting over the water, and played tag down a wooded path, they engaged in a real-world reality check. They absorbed a truth that cannot be improved upon. Joy and health seeped into their beings.

When I go outside and work in the garden, when I take a walk down a country road, when I sit and chat face-to-face with someone, even a stranger, I engage in a real-world reality that cannot be replaced by any technological gadget.

I wonder if that is why some television programs have become so weird. They are reflecting that absence, that disconnect, that xeroxed print, which has been copied too often and become anemic and a little warped in the process.

Perhaps what our teens need is a little more time with natural reality, not "reality shows." Perhaps writers should reflect human beings in our real world and not slapstick, word-bites meant merely to get a laugh or jerk a tear.

Reality—our real world—isn't meant to lead to suicide.

Prayer, Work, Study
Originally published on The Writings of A. K. Frailey 3/5/2016

A balanced life is an opportunity to live to our fullest potential. I love the monastic ideal of dividing the day between the three core needs of our lives: prayer, work, and study.

As a family, we punctuate our day with prayer in the morning, at noon, and in the evening. Of course, I am frequently tossing prayers up to heaven for a variety of daily mini-disasters or concerns. Yesterday, some of the kids and I spent an hour in Adoration. It was one of the fastest hours of my life. There is a lot to pray for in this world of ours, and it is wonderful that we have such a loving God to call upon, knowing that He will listen and respond. The key to joyful prayer is to allow God to be God and not set Him by our clocks.

Work is also a large part of our day. Today three of the kids helped a neighbor to gather in a hefty wood supply. We all helped to stack the wood, so it'll be dried and ready for next winter. A couple of the kids worked on planting seeds for the spring garden, and one of the kids made zucchini bread. Everyone worked hard today. Everyone will sleep well tonight.

And finally, study is one of the most enjoyable activities of the day. Each of the kids has a full curriculum to draw from, but book learning isn't the only kind of learning that matters. We also learn by responding to daily needs. Learning to cook, to fix broken tools, to take care of animals, to organize our supplies for the year, to balance a budget are all invaluable learning experiences. It is fun to study history, to read and write, to tease out a math problem, but learning is like breathing, it happens without even knowing it. It's important to make sure that we offer information and skills that improve and inspire our lives rather than being dragged down by the negative influences around us.

A balanced life of prayer, work, and study have been the best recipe for joy and contentment in our lives.

The Million-Faceted Crystal
Originally published on The Writings of A. K. Frailey 4/2/2016
Guest post by Teresa Frailey

In Charles Dickens' *Tale of Two Cities*, Chapter Three, entitled: *The Night Shadows*, he wrote, "*A wonderful fact to reflect upon, that every human creature is constituted to be that profound secret and mystery to every other. A solemn consideration, when I enter a great city by night, that every one of those darkly clustered houses encloses its own secret; that every room in every one of them encloses its own secret; that every beating heart in the hundreds of thousands of breasts there, is, in some of its imaginings, a secret to the heart nearest it! Something of the awfulness, even of Death itself, is preferable to this.*"

Dickens struck upon an integral characteristic of humanity, that every beating heart is the greatest quandary to its companions. The uniqueness of each human person far exceeds the design of a thumbprint. The human person (rational animal or not) is a mystery that would take, I think, an eternity to unravel.

Dickens' words strike a deep chord in me. The fact that we can see only through our own eyes is a somewhat mind-boggling consideration. The image of a city at night, filled with tens of thousands of unique hearts, paints a spectacular image. It makes me think of the human heart as a diamond, or crystal, with a million facets. We show particular faces to particular people. But when all is said and done, even our best friend will, at times, still marvel at the mystery of who we are.

Two Brains in One and Sleep Deprivation
Originally published on The Writings of A. K. Frailey 6/11/2016

Soooo, speaking of sleep deprivation... We *were* speaking of sleep deprivation, weren't we? Since it feels like my obsession these days, we must've been.

Why do our days have to get looonger right when summer rolls around and the garden needs to be tended—on top of a kazillion other things that need to be done in the course of a day? Does the sun care? Does it take any moral responsibility for the fact that the human race is scurrying about in frantic haste on the surface of the third planet, wearing themselves to a frazzle because the saying, "*Make hay why the sun shines.*" Seems to make some kind of relative sense to our benumbed, exhausted, and guilt-ridden minds?

Silence.

Just as I suspected, the sun's not fessing up to anything. Yeah, I know, it's summer somewhere on the planet all the time. That doesn't really help.

I just watched **You Are Two—CGP Grey** and found myself having one of those "Aha!" moments. So. The right brain is our silent partner? Yeah, sure. I doubt it is so silent. I suspect that silent right brain is really the brains behind the weird dream sequences, which inform us of the *real* state of our mind and the impending psychotic break we like to pretend isn't happening.

You know what I am talking about. Those dreams where the kitchen broom has grown to statue-of-liberty-size and chases us down the halls of our childhood home, which bizarrely looks a lot like our fifth-grade classroom. Obviously, Right Brain is having some fun with us after a day of being hammered with twenty kazillion images/problems/paradoxes and only three rational choices.

So, we have two brains in one person?

My son wondered if that was anything like the Trinity, three persons in one God.

Right Brain, any thoughts on that?

Oh, yeah, you'll let me know—tonight.

Sunrise Paradox
Originally published on The Writings of A. K. Frailey 5/24/2018

Picture a sunrise or a sunset—whichever you prefer.
Its beauty can bring the human soul to its knees.

Now go higher...

The Earth is round. In fact, the sun is setting and the sun is rising every moment of every day.

The sun has risen.
The sun has set.
The sun is rising.
The sun is setting.
Now, go higher...

The sun is fixed in space. It has never risen. It has never set.

The sun has risen.
The sun has set.
The sun is rising.
The sun is setting.
The sun has never risen or set.
So much depends on where we are. What we perceive

.

My Kind of Madness
Originally published on The Writings of A. K. Frailey 6/6/2018

Over time, I've become convinced that madness must run in the family. How else can I explain my insane desire to "live simply," which, by necessity, involves all sorts of discomforts from merely annoying insects to knockdown drag-out encounters with the wild side of creation? Whoever said nature was innocent, never met nature up close and personal.

My husband and I both grew up in cities. He, in Los Angeles, I, in Milwaukee. We both traveled and knew "something of the world" before we met and married. Thankfully, we both came to the conclusion that we wanted to raise our kids in the country. Images of blissful encounters with nature and the soul-steadying reality of hard work encouraged us to forge ahead with what would become a lot more intense experience than we could have ever realized.

But that was good. Otherwise, we would've never done it. God isn't stupid when He doesn't color in all the details. Oh, no.

Luckily, John was very strong and loved nature. He was soon dubbed "Our Amish Paul Bunyan" by the homeschooling dads. Good thing because I was rather busy having babies. Eight babies. Yes. One at a time.

During those years, we learned to raise laying hens for eggs, meat birds for our winter chicken supply, maintain a humongous garden, raise bees and gather the honey. Each spring, John collected sap from the maple trees and made maple syrup. That was fun. Kids around a huge cauldron over an open fire in the backyard, stirring…and stirring…and stirring. And then pancakes. Life was good.

We got a cow and learned to milk it. Or, rather, my eldest daughter did. I hid with the chickens. But I did learn to make cheese. Sort of. Okay, my homemade bread was eatable, though.

We are the kind of people who drive other people nuts. We don't use air conditioning—unless you have a heart condition or are with social services. We actually like to recycle. All the kids work. Or else. Pretty much everyone collapses on Sunday. No need for a "Though shalt rest" commandment. God knows what He's doing.

When John was diagnosed with leukemia, our youngest was only seven months. There was no way I could do everything. So I didn't. I simply did what I could. The kids did what they could. John did what he could—till he couldn't do anything. But those joint efforts—raising the chickens, milking the cow, making cheese (sort of), gardening—they did a lot to keep the rhythm of our lives going even when our hearts were skipping beats.

John died in December 2013, and since then, the kids and I have struggled to maintain the core of our little natural world. I can't really call it a farm. We have loosey-goosy hens that lay eggs in the doghouse, meat birds that die without asking, and bees we watch but do not follow, a middle-sized garden, fruit trees, nut trees, and more dogs and cats than I care to count. Don't ask about the possums and assorted critters that like to visit. We do chat on occasion. I tell them to go home. They ignore me.

When things get tough and I'm ready to give up on one more thing, I remember why John and I started this foolishness in the first place. There is something sublime about working hard and living according to your conscience. Nature isn't always easy, but in the fruits, vegetables, nuts, critters, weather, and the land itself, we see daily facets of God's abundant imagination.

We learn balance and integrity while working with God's created world. Jesus spoke in nature parables all the time. We are stewards. If we're not ever vigilant, weeds will destroy our garden.

There's nothing quite like the blessings of hard physical labor, homemade bread and strawberry jam. It isn't the amount of land worked, the number of chickens raised, the variety of critters encountered. It's the interaction. The noticing...the caring...the faithfulness needed to keep everyone alive. We are known by our fruit.

It's my kind of madness.

Turning Points
Originally published on The Writings of A. K. Frailey 8/28/2018

I was driving along a long stretch of country highway today, golden corn waving at me from each side, Italian music playing—not mine, my daughter's. I don't know Italian, but I enjoy the beat, nonetheless. Maybe more. I feel the emotion without being told what to think.

And as I swerve around ka-billion woolly-worms maniacally crossing the road, I notice out of the corner of my eye a long gravel driveway guarded by stone lions.

But that's not what stops my heart. Between the stone lions is a little girl dressed in what must be her best dress—very colorful—dancing to her heart's content.

I had just finished reading Michael Tabb's new book, *Prewriting Your Screenplay*, and I had reread the section on turning points.

Characters in books and movies aren't the only ones who have turning points. You. Me. The guy in line ahead of you at the store. The cafeteria lady at school. The UPS delivery person. You know what I'm talking about. Those moments that catch our eye—and our heart—and make us pause. Make us think. Make us feel.

What did I feel as I raced (not speeding) along the road, my heart beating to the rhythm of an Italian pop singer? I felt courage. The courage of whoever the heck put up those stone lions in the first place. The courage of a child dancing for all the world to see. The courage of farmers throughout the ages, daring to plant crops, no matter what the weather and the world might throw at them.

In our fractured world, knit together by the flick of a computer cursor, we have to hold our courage in our hands every day. What turning point caught your eye this week? What heartbeat touched yours?

Do I really care? Yep.

Picture Perfect
Originally published on The Writings of A. K. Frailey 9/4/2018

One of my favorite mom things to do is to read to my kids. When they were little, I especially loved reading books with detailed pictures—pictures that are real-er than real, if you know what I mean. Tasha Tudor was one of those artists who created art that lifted mundane realities into the Heavenly Spheres.

This morning when I looked around my kitchen, (the one I left pretty darn clean the night before.) I saw...a coffee spoon and a dribble of coffee on the counter, a splotch of jam on the floor, a spider web in the window (with a spider, no less!), and a vase of withered flowers on the table.

And there, lying on a chair, sat Tasha's book.

As if I had nothing in the world better to do, I opened it and glanced at her world for a moment...or twenty.

By the time I lifted my eyes and looked at my kitchen again, it had magically changed. I saw well-fed school children engrossed in a new book... happy coffee-ed college kids heading off to educational adventures, an arachnid ally taking a bit of rest after a long night's work, and the glory of late summer wildflowers (granted—a little worse for wear) plucked by loving hands.

I suppose there are a lot of ways of looking at our world. And though it is a parent's duty to keep an orderly house, there is something to be said for seeing the kitchen...and the living room...and...(fill in the blank) with an artist's eye.

I suspect Tasha would agree.

In a Wider Universe
Originally published on The Writings of A. K. Frailey 9/8/2018

Writing is a lot like praying.

When I pray, I reach out toward the luminous and mysterious God who created me, trusting that He hears my voice.

When I write, I reach out to unnamed readers—through eternal time, to all corners of the world—hoping that my splintered fragment of reality will resonate with our shared humanity.

When I wrote the first version of *ARAM*, I visualized a basic human truth: There is a God. We are not Him. That was enough to get me started.

In Ishtar's story, I moved deeper into our relationship with the supernatural world, involving the reality of good and evil, repentance and healing.

Finally, in Neb's history, I combatted the reality of fallen souls—those who chose through free will to abandon the God who created them—and their descendants who must live with the consequences.

Though the stories effectively represented core human struggles, they did not reach out to the wider universe. In the intervening years since I wrote my first novel, the world has grown closer through the Internet and modern technology, yet sadly, also more polarized. In adding the science fiction universe to the OldEarth world, which I first conceptualized in my Newearth series, I drew the universality of the human experience into a tighter weave.

Being human isn't what makes us truly great. Being created by the same God defines our glory. We search the stars for signs of life—do aliens exist? Are angels not aliens created by God so vastly different from ourselves that we only glimmer hints of their reality? Aliens or angels, human beings struggle with our identity and purpose of existence, the supernatural world, and our choices involving good and evil.

In the OldEarth Encounter series, the questions do not change; they simply get asked in a wider universe. Sometimes, we see things more clearly from a distance.

If you're interested in delving into a world—both old and new—feel free to pick up one of the OldEarth encounter novels or one from the Newearth series.

We are not alone.

We come from God.

Blanket Personalities

Originally published on The Writings of A. K. Frailey 9/18/2018

Blankets have personalities.

Literally.

I'm not talking about some highfalutin metaphorical image of our broken world. I'm talking about the strange personalities our blankets and sheets take on at night while we are in our weakest state, unable to properly defend ourselves. If you're deeply honest, you'll recognize your own blanket's personality here.

First, there's the most common—what I call the *slithering personality*. Not to be stereotypical about sheets, but I do believe more bed coverings slip into this category than any other. The night starts off optimistically enough. You get on your PJs, slide under the coverlet, read your book till you're nice and drowsy (certain books accomplish this better than others), and fall asleep with your sheets and blanket nicely positioned.

But then...you awake shivering. Grasping confusedly, you find your supposed friend and nighttime ally, slumped on the floor to the right or left, or (in extremely embarrassing situations) at the foot of the bed. After a bit of a tussle, you punch a little life into the fabric and spread it out, encouraging words tangled up with grunts and slight aspersions to the sheet's quality. Once set, you try again...and again... But by morning, there it lay in a heap, looking just as miserable as you feel—as you rub your eyes in exhaustion.

Second, there's what I fondly refer to the *enchiladas-lover personality*. You find yourself waking up completely stiff, unable to move, wrapped up as tight as King Tut's mummy. Sheets have been known to accomplish this maneuver just as well as blankets. Personally, I think they are tied for honors here. It's a difficult situation to manage and not get caught in mid-stream. It's an even more difficult situation to get out of. If they're really good, they get both your arms wrapped up tight against your body while you are face down. Top points! Marks off for leaving one arm free or being loosey-goosey in the middle.

Third and finally, there's the *nefarious personality* in which a blanket likes to congregate around the head, pretending that he's keeping the mosquitoes off your face, but you have your doubts, as it's nearly twenty below zero outside. Though the initial "head covering" is the most common maneuver of this personality type, they have been known to attempt strangulation by wrapping themselves about the neck. Once caught, they fall limp in your hands, as if the thought of anything ominous never entered their fibers. Beware of this kind...they're sneaky and highly proficient sleep stealers. After all, who in their right mind can get any rest after such an encounter?

So there you have three inescapable blanket personalities. Not being a particularly worldly person, my catalog is naturally quite small. Perhaps you've met a few other types? Feel free to send me a note about those you've encountered. I really ought to write a scientific book labeling them all properly (in Latin?) for posterity's sake.

Maybe then I'd get some sleep.

Love
Originally published on The Writings of A. K. Frailey 9/25/2018

I love...a lot of things. Today, as I picked the last tomatoes off the vine, I was reminded how much I love fresh fruits and vegetables. When I dropped my son off at a neighbor's house to do yard work and chatted with a neighbor lady who just celebrated her 100th year anniversary with her husband (okay, that's a slight exaggeration), I thought about sustained marital love and all the hills and valley's that kind of love must endure. Then, later, as I connected with a mother of seven kids, I thought about moms and how their love changes yet always remains the same.

I often don't realize how much I love people or things until they are on the brink of extinction or gone entirely. How human is that?

As passionate beings, we associate love with physical sensations: hot-spiced cider, the fragrance of flowers, a glorious sunset, the music score of our favorite movie, the touch of a loved one. But real love—the one that lasts from one season to another—must travel from physical reality to a secret place in our souls.

Soon, the garden will sleep in winter's embrace. Even the most delicious meal must come to an end. Perfumes dissipate. Children grow up and move away. Friends and family pass to the other side.

Some days, we stand silent, alone, in the dark.

But deep inside, I know that the garden, the honeysuckle blossoms, hot cocoa, homemade bread, friendly neighbors, loving parents, happy children, and the warm embrace of loving hearts still live.

Along with the God who made them all—the One who loves me, forever and always, in His secret place

Should Old Acquaintance Be Forgot
...and never thought upon...
Originally published on The Writings of A. K. Frailey 10/2/2018

It's hard to look back and remember. Two dates in October stand out for me, the birthdates of two people I loved who have passed on: my mother and my husband.

It should be uncomplicated. I loved them. They died. Be grateful. Accept. Move on.

But when is life uncomplicated? There are a host of reasons why memories of loved ones haunt us. Mistakes they made. Mistakes we made. The whole death process. Our own impending death. Our existence here. Their existence...where?

I've been studying up on my Irish heritage. Of course, that can't be simple either. My DNA reflects Irish, English, Scottish, Scandinavian, Iberian Peninsula... Lord, my ancestors were passionate travelers. History references all sorts of lost longings...the people and communities we once belonged to. The families we had...or wished we had.

So when I write the date on the chalkboard for the kids each day, do I include a reminder...this was grandma's birthday? Your dad's birthday? Of course. Right? We should remember. Selectively.

Relationships are hard even when we aren't together anymore. That's the irony of it all. We can't really forget. Sometimes, we'd like to. There's a lot we'd like to purge from our psyche. After all, we only have so much brain space, and we can only carry so much emotional baggage. Right?

So why is it that the tune to the words—words we don't even remember half the time—brings tears to our eyes? Why do we make resolutions on New Year's Day? Why do we try so hard to start over?

Not being a cultural engineer with all the right answers or human rights activist with all the right causes or even a particularly good mirror...I struggle with these questions.

Why am I here?

And where do I go from here?

Though I may not have the answers, I believe they are worthy questions to ponder. That's why the song brings a lump to my throat and tears to my eyes.

It's a good question.

Human Journey
Originally published on The Writings of A. K. Frailey 10/9/2018

I pulled into a gas station the other day practically on autopilot, filled the car with gasoline, paid the attendant, and started on my way. As I turned to go, I noticed a woman sitting in the car opposite me on the driver's side with the door open, one leg extended as if she planned to get out but had stopped in mid-motion.

Since a truck blocked my way, I had to wait. So I looked over, ever so slightly concerned. Was she ill?

Nope.

She sat there, composed, but looking up into the sky as if she could see the limitless recesses of an unimagined universe. But that universe didn't appear to be doing too well. Not by the expression on her face.

A flicker of doubt swept over me. Should I be that well-meaning do-gooder and ask if she was all right?

The truck moved on, and my way was clear. I glanced back, but she hadn't moved. Her eyes were glued to the sky. Coward though I may be, I decided to leave her to her musings...memories...grief or whatever she was experiencing. It looked very much like a private moment, even though she was in the middle of a gas station.

I've learned through hard experience that I can't "save" everyone. Honestly, I shouldn't even try. I once attempted to assist a bleeding man on the streets of L. A. and got only the man's irritation and a medic's scorn for my effort. Not that I was wrong to make the attempt...I was simply wrong for being so certain that he wanted my help. He didn't.

Most often, I've found that people who want help will ask for it. I can always ask to assist, but gently, and with respect for an honest no.

The one thing I can do without much fuss is pray. God knows what we need—better than we know ourselves. So I prayed for the woman. She may have been basking in a lovely memory for all I know. Or her heart may have been breaking.

But I do know that the closer we embrace God, the more beautifully we embrace each other. I pulled out of the gas station and drove home, aware once again of the secret depth of each human's journey story. We pass each other as we drive by on highways and byways, we steer our carts around each other at the grocery store, we sit next to each other at countless offices, and we barely look each other in the eye.

There are moments when we can save each other—heroically or quietly—but at least, in the passing events of each day, we can always pray for each other.

Getting Educated
Originally published on The Writings of A. K. Frailey 10/16/2018

I took a pot of tea and a plate of banana bread to my ninety-year-old neighbor this week. Her eyesight is not what it used to be, so I figured she was feeling a little lonesome without the comfortable companionship of her daily allotment of newspaper stories and books. Her farmer sons are as attentive as busy farmer's sons can be during harvest season. So, when she called to chat, I suggested a cup of English Tea and a "little something" to go along with our chat.

She was amiable to the idea.

Not that our little town keeps us in gossip, but there's always someone who has gone to the hospital and could use a prayer, or a highlight on recent coupon finds, a memory to peruse, grandkids' news to catch up on, new pictures to check out, and possible remedies for what ails you to try.

God has always blessed me with elderly ladies. There's always been a neighbor—somewhere—to spend an hour or two with. I love sitting by and listening to stories that no one else wants to hear, laughing about how the world has changed, and remarking at how, in fact, the world really hasn't changed all that much.

Disease, accident, or a quick death will find me sooner or later. I'm not under the illusion that I'll live in peace and prosperity forever. Not on this side of the Great Divide. So getting to know my elderly friends is like a life lesson in how to handle the inevitable challenges—weakness, failing eyesight, loss of hearing, loneliness, bittersweet memories, and so much more.

My friend says she wants to educate me because I'm dreadfully deficient in coupon savvy. I don't seem to know the four cardinal directions or how to properly clean a window. I waste money on needless supplies when—with a little time and effort—I could make something like the store-bought kind from scratch. I also don't save used envelopes. When it comes to molding me into a proper country housewife, she certainly has her work cut out. And nothing could please her more. Or me, for that matter.

We have a cacophony of authoritative voices shrieking at us all day long from newscasts to blog posts (hopefully, not this one!) informing us of how to live right. How to make the world a better place. How to become strong, beautiful, holy, and helpful.

Yep. The world offers lots of great advice.

But no one makes me laugh like my friend.

No Guts, No Glory
Originally published on The Writings of A. K. Frailey 10/23/2018

There I was, getting into my car on the wrong side. The passenger's side. One of my sons slid behind the wheel, put the key in the ignition, and pulled onto our country road. To say that I was nervous would be an understatement. Try settling inside a two-ton metal box and give a teen the controls and see how you feel. Speed praying becomes second nature. Trust me.

At the time, I was a recent widow and facing more unknowns than Captain Kirk in one of Star Trek's newest uncharted galaxies. Teaching my two sons to drive was just one more in a long, snaky line of impossible tasks.

It wasn't until the end of their driving classes, around early spring, that one of my boys informed me of my late husband's pronouncement every time he got in the car with them. He'd say, "No guts, no glory." Then, he'd promptly fall asleep and let the boys handle the driving.

I nearly choked. If John had been alive, I might have choked him.

But as the season rotated on their usual sublime schedule and the boys passed their drivers' tests and became excellent drivers, I learned how to fix mechanical thingamajigs without the use of duct tape, and life rolled on into full summer glory full of birdsong, I realized something rather important.

John was right.

This Side of the Divide
Originally published on The Writings of A. K. Frailey 10/30/2018

I'm sitting in a parking lot waiting for my daughter to come out of her catechism class and my sons to finish their altar boy training session. It's only Wednesday, but it's already been a long week. World-weariness troubles my soul.

You too?

I can almost hear your sigh.

It seems that fresh scandals break every week: religious, political, and culture wars lash out at every level of society.

With the disheartening reality of broken humanity and the faithful losing their faith, it seems odd to be joining more church-related activities these days. According to current trends, I should be pulling away disgusted. Isolated. Disillusioned.

But I have the ridiculous habit of reading history books. And if you pay attention to the past, certain things stand out as trends throughout the ever-lengthening ages. Broken humanity is one of them. Apparently, it's not a new trend at all.

I don't teach my children religion to save them from grief or to give them all the right answers. I teach them the Catholic faith because it is a healing hope in a world full of grieving hearts.

Jesus certainly knew a thing or two about sin-laden people, confused mindsets, weak wills, and pierced hearts. His mom must have known it too. After the religious authorities of her day murdered her innocent son using the laws of the established church to do so, she still followed the traditions of her faith and waited until after the Sabbath to anoint his body. The body that wasn't there. The body that rose beyond all reason and grief.

Faith is a lot like hope. It isn't reasonable. It doesn't protect itself at all costs. Love embraces both the faithful and the despairing, strengthens the will, holds up exhausted arms, and heals even the most mortally pierced heart.

The evening bells are ringing...a haunting sound on a late autumn evening. The bells toll for us all. Time passes, and each of us is called. Every day. To the voice of grief and desperation. To the clarion call of change. To the herald of a new day. To the whisper of a spirit that has been—is now—and always will be.

I can't define or even defend God. That's His job.

I just love Him. Passionately. Faithfully. And with a renewed soul.

Some Days I Wonder
Originally published on The Writings of A. K. Frailey 11/20/2018

After school today, I took a few of the kids to the local thrift store. One-stop shopping you might say, as they have a variety of goods. Excellent for kids on a limited budget and moms perfectly aware of pre-teen boy's track record with jeans, coats, and anything that can be used in an imaginary world where barbarians play a significant role. We got what we needed, paid our dues, which felt a lot like stealing, and headed out with our clumpy bundle.

Next stop, the local bookstore. Trigger alert. I'm about to describe a real bookstore. A large room with high ceilings, peeling paint, drooping wallpaper, and lots of books. When I say, "lots of books," I mean there is not an uncovered surface in the entire place. There are book racks on every wall, shelves of books all the way to the glorious heights, tables with stacks upon stacks of books, counters covered in piles of books, towers of books on the floor every few feet, and if it were possible, I'm nearly certain that books would hang from the ceiling like geometric stalactites.

The miraculous thing? Yep. You guessed it. We found our literary hearts' desires in only a matter of minutes. I used to be a bit of a neat freak, and my late husband's untidy habits left me cold and breathless. It was one of those—accept what you can't change—sort of things. But, lo and behold, give me five years running the homestead, and I'm quickly learning that a certain level of mess is good for the soul. Who knew?

A harrowing drive along narrow country roads at dusk with Sci-fi-Sears-Tower-sized tractors rounding every bend, and we made it home. And, no, I wasn't speeding. Not so as anyone would notice.

Time to make a delicious meatloaf...and, while I'm at it, I'll just wipe down the refrigerator. What on God's green Earth compelled me to such action, I hardly know. I had plenty of worthy things to do. I could write tomorrow's spelling words on the chalkboard, work on my next novel, find the solution to human misery, but, no, instead, I decided to pull out the refrigerator drawers. And shelves. And what did I come slap face-to-face with?

Yep, you guessed it. Dante's Inferno.

So, as the meatloaf did its thing inside the oven, (which had done a self-cleaning yesterday. No little scrubbing arms—I was rather disappointed), I tackled the refrigerator. Scrubbing goo off plastic has never been a highlight of my day. But I figured I might as well make the most of it. But instead of whistling, I found myself remembering snatches of a book I read years ago—*Men are from Mars and Women Are from Venus.*

My mental state degenerated from there. I found myself asking the six-foot appliance why it had hidden this mess from me. I had been faithful, wiping it down every week, clearing out odoriferous leftovers promptly. So what was the deal? Why hit me with all this back-of-the-drawer, hidden-behind-shelves stuff now?

This past year, I realized I've been hit with several relationship blowouts. Not unlike the bulb that exploded when I merely tapped it with a wet rag. Granted, with the hot glass and the damp rag, I deserved what I got. But with humans in my midst, I was completely taken by surprise. Didn't see the rupture coming. Until I looked back. Then I saw all the obvious signs and wondered how I had managed to be so blind. So much for whistling. Only in the dark at this point.

So now, it's time for prayers and (I-pray-to-God) a good night's rest. But I can't escape from the reality of my day. Lessons learned. Challenges faced. Goo removed.

Some days I wonder what's in store for me. But I figure—I'll get up anyway.

A Deep Moral Dilemma
Originally published on The Writings of A. K. Frailey 11/27/2018

An old farmer friend called today and asked if I wanted my annual bales of straw. Since the dogs and cats seem to appreciate the snug houses my kids build for them each autumn, I maintained my routine. My friend is the kind of person that I'm convinced that if more people acted like him, angels could retire. Uncomplicated but thoughtful. Honest yet self-effacing. He'll never take money for the bales. Though thankfully, he will take jars of homemade pickles, salsa, and jam.

Near the end of our "How's life treating you?" conversation, which naturally canvasses the weather, family, and sublime universal themes, he asked if I needed any wood this winter. To be honest, I wasn't sure what to say. Seemed like a simple question, but it involved a deep moral dilemma.

When my late husband and I moved out to the country, we hadn't a fig's newton what we were doing. We were both city people and the idea of raising children in the country seemed so terribly healthy and right. So—you know—natural. Turns out—it sure is. But nature is nothing to be sniffed at.

John being John, he did all the muscle work, and I did the other stuff. House management. Finances. Kid care. Education. We made an excellent team. We were practically Amish in our desire to keep everything as natural as possible. As close to home as possible. As holistic as possible. We were going to "steward" our world, not destroy it.

After his death, I continued our long-standing traditions. So far as I was able. A few things changed, though. The bees have had to manage on their own, and I've about given up reasoning with the hens. They lay wherever the huff they want to, and good luck finding the eggs before the dogs do.

But before my friend called today, the kids and I had been watching a documentary on JRR Tolkien. At one point, his son, Christopher, described Tolkien's severe dislike for machinery, and my mouth about dropped to the floor. How familiar—that sense that man-made takes us away from God-made. Except in the case of washing machines, of course. Washing machines are a divine gift to the human race. Try washing eight sets of kids' clothes by hand, and you'll see what I mean.

Getting older myself and having kids who keep adding years to their ages at an alarming rate, I realized that perhaps our woodstove would become another casualty of "Things-That-Just-Can't-Be-Managed." I like the woodstove because the heat feels warmer and because, like the garden, it takes healthy work. I'm more sensitive to the weather and the natural world around me because I have to plan ahead if a cold blast or a storm is coming. The kids have to fill the stick boxes. Wood has its own lovely scent, rough texture, and can smash your fingers if you're not careful. I wasn't ready to let the woodstove go, but I honestly couldn't scrounge off my friend or chop down the scanty woods we have around here. So I explained that I'd love to keep the woodstove going, but...

Turns out, my friend has a friend who sells wood at a reasonable price and even delivers. Reprieve! Tendrils of wood smoke will still grace our chimney this winter.

I certainly appreciate Tolkien's view on machines...though I've made peace with more hardware than I'd like to admit. Still, I think he had a point...and my younger, less-worn-out self had a point, too. Nature-made tools and materials speak to a part of our humanity that we often abandon for more efficient manmade tools. They demand a level of attentiveness and care that comfort seekers might find irritating.

Yet I can't ignore the fact that my critters abandon their plastic igloos and snuggle up in their straw bale abodes every winter, and nothing beats the cheery glow, embracing warmth, and crackle of a wood fire on a cold evening. Perhaps I feel this way because I, too, am naturally God made...

Beyond Words
Originally published on The Writings of A. K. Frailey 12/4/2018

As I sat in the Chapel at Greenville University on Sunday evening, I realized for the ka-billionth time that though our music on Earth may not exactly transport us to Heaven, it certainly builds a beautiful bridge.

This is the second year I've encountered The Greenville Choral Union and Orchestra, and this time they not only played selections from The Messiah but also beautiful compositions in Russian, Nigerian, and Spanish.

As I sat in the packed room, two college kids in front of me swayed to the rhythm, an assembly of older folks listened in rapt attention, and couples joined hands. Even small children stopped squirming. A remarkable feat in this technology-dominated era.

The glory of the voices mingling as an intertwining chorus and the skill of the musicians drew my attention to sublime realities.

One major thought that struck me was the sheer cooperation that had to take place for such an event to happen. There must have been well over fifty musicians and support people who set this evening as a priority in their lives, arranged their schedules, their families' schedules, and accomplished all the seriously hard work to prepare for the occasion. For faith-filled music? And considering this was a donation event, it's clear they weren't doing it for the big bucks.

As I listened, I imagined different places in the world at the same moment in our shared human history. A God's-eye view, perhaps. I thought of all the Illinois families trying to put their lives into some sort of order after the recent tornadoes, the Alaskan families struggling with the massive damage due to the recent earthquake, various people across the globe—some living in squalor, some sleeping in soft beds, and some suffering from addictions, violence, and terror.

But the music played on. The glorious sounds stretched beyond our globe of human pain and suffering—and for a couple hours—some of us knew peace, joy, and pure gratitude.

I can't help but believe—for that moment—God knew it too.

It's not often that humanity offers a perfect gift to God, but the Greenville University Choral Union gave a supreme effort. On behalf of humanity, I'm grateful.

Beyond words.

Surprise Me
Originally published on The Writings of A. K. Frailey 12/11/2018

Sometimes I like to joke around with God. When trying to predict how something will turn out, I imagine all sorts of scenarios and feel pretty certain that nothing I imagine is even close to what will actually happen. Knowing this, I tell God, "Go ahead and surprise me."

He does.

This has already proven to be a colder, snowier winter than I expected, so when I had to drive an hour away to take the kids to an appointment, I prepared for the worst. But in fact, the roads were perfectly clear, and the drive was easy.

What I wasn't prepared for was the waiting room. Or rather the Kafkaesque reality therein.

The television—front and center—was blaring the latest news. Gloom and Doom. Isn't it always? Lots of conflicts, doubt, and innuendo. I fully expect the news commentators to throw up their hands one of these days and screech, "Head for the hills; the sky is falling!"

I pulled out my book and tried to shut out the flat-screen horror. But…

To the left of me, a teen decided that it was time to quiz her mom on Spanish vocabulary, despite the fact that the mom kept insisting that she didn't know any Spanish. The kid's pronunciation was poor, so I could hardly blame the mother for not understanding her even if she did speak Spanish. But what caught me off guard was the kid's snarkasm. New word. Like it? She was so snarkastic that she practically filled the small space with her snarality.

I crouched tighter over my book and pulled my coat up around my ears. Blinders. I thought that might help.

It didn't.

Directly in front of me—just hovering over my book edge—a young couple huddled in glorious love. Glorious, except for the small fact that we were in the middle of a medium-sized waiting room. A strangled attempt to clear my throat never touched their consciousness.

And to the left of me...a young guy played with a bright, shiny, flashing arcade. Personally, I think he was almost as deeply impassioned as the snuggling couple before me. His bouncing, bopping, chattering to every mechanical ding and ring altered my sense of the human-machine divide. Apparently, some humans have crossed into new dimensions.

I've been blind. Again.

As I drove home, I relished the idea of retreating into my safe and snug little home world. Though I have to admit, I realize more than ever that my understanding of humanity is often based on fantasy and is nothing close to reality. I read books and watch a few programs and expect certain real-world scenarios to go according to a scripted formula. When they don't, I'm a bit flummoxed.

I suspect God's having a bit of fun with me. I worry about my kids driving on the roads. I scheme and plan for special events. I pray my heart out for certain causes. Sometimes, things go flat, and I'm disappointed. Sometimes, terror strikes, and I have to hold on to my courage. Sometimes, I'm amazed by the richness and breathtaking joy of God's vision, which turns into reality I could never have planned for or imagined in my wildest dreams.

All in all, I'm glad I went out in the cold and snow and sat in that waiting room. I could have avoided it by staying at home. Living in my safe, imaginary world. But then I wouldn't really be living...

Walk On Water
Originally published on The Writings of A. K. Frailey 12/18/2018

As I grow older...though not necessarily wiser...I gain more experience on which to base my judgments. So it's not completely irrational that I think I know what I'm doing most of the time. The operative word here is "most."

I discovered recently that I had completely misjudged someone based on past experiences. Usually, I give people the benefit of the doubt using my trusty default nice streak. But at the time, I wasn't in any mood to do that.

Granted, there had been a host of disappointments that set my trust-o-meter to sub-zero, but still, this person carried not an ounce of responsibility for other people's failures.

As my life—with truth and lies unfolding—becomes more complex, my world shifts, and my vision blurs. As I pondered my past mistakes, I realized that misjudgments are probably more often the case than not. It's hard to judge myself accurately, much less anyone else. It's impossible to climb into someone's head, peer down into the heart, search out motives, and clear away all the emotional clutter we carry around inside, burying our better selves or hiding behind chosen perfection.

So, in all humility, where can I turn? Who will understand and not judge me for a mere fool? Who sees beyond my excuses and takes an honest look at how I behaved?

In the end, I turn to the One who has much better eyesight than I do. One who can peer into my self-centered mind, my protective heart, my overzealous soul and take me where I actually stand. In surrendering myself to God, I have found peace. I've also discovered that I can accept the mystery of other people a bit better. That doesn't mean I accept evil as good. But the controlling—save myself, others, and the whole blinking world—part of me has loosened its grip.

I don't know what will happen tomorrow. Good heaven! I don't even know what will happen this afternoon. But I'm getting a little more comfortable with that fact...that uncertainty. Reality has consequences. Jump from a cliff without wings, and you'll likely die. Lie, cheat, steal, treat other human beings as toys...and the taunts of hell will trip your every step.

In a world where everyone seems like an expert—I'm okay being uncertain about some things. I'm glad that God is God. I don't want His job. I've got to make a semblance of a sense of the struggling-to-survive world in front of me. This human journey is a labyrinth fraught with peril, and our choices can have eternal consequences. Yet we must live. We must make decisions. We must keep walking. On water. So it seems.

That seems to be the key. If we're going to join the mystery of God and trust Him with our frail humanity, we have to walk on water.

Just keep walking.

Well Lived
Originally published on The Writings of A. K. Frailey 12/25/2018

My youngest son decided to reorganize his room today, and when I went to check, I saw that he had piled a stack of box springs and mattresses on top of each other to rival something out of The Princess and the Pea. He called it King Sized. Yep. I'd say so. I swallowed and merely asked him not to fall off in the middle of the night and break himself into Humpty-Dumpty pieces. He assured me he'd be careful.

I had a sudden memory of the first time one of my boys climbed a tree, reaching what my mother's heart considered dizzying heights. I knew at the time that climbing trees was a normal pastime for kids—I had climbed plenty in my day—but still, I had the urge to ask him to get back to earth. An urge I resisted.

Later, as I plodded up the steps with my umpteenth load of laundry, I noticed that my formerly clean counter was now hosting what looked like a rather odd science experiment involving toothpaste, shampoo, and baking soda. I didn't even ask. Just waved my hand in a "You know what you'll be doing when you're done—right?" attitude. "Please don't spill it all over the floor" didn't even need to be verbalized.

Sometimes, I wonder what a stranger might think if he or she wandered into our home on any ordinary day. It's generally quiet, though the piano is played quite a bit. Holidays and birthdays are celebrated in style with a cleaning frenzy right before. With laughter.

But more often than not, there are piles of books here and there. Pencils and papers scattered about. Drawings half-finished on the couch. Knitting projects proudly ensconced on a living room chair. Woodworking projects clutter the basement floor. Broken floor tiles skitter underfoot. Light smoke from the wood stoves tints the walls. A couple door handles are loose.

It is a well-used house. The kitchen sink is practically never empty, even though I (and the kids) do dishes the live-long day. The washer and dryer have given us their hearts and souls several times over. Footsteps patter upstairs or down the steps constantly. A door opens and shuts like a heartbeat.

We are not living in a magazine. Nor would I want to. The kids learn from taking their room apart and building glorious beds. They see new heights from the tops of trees. They practice drawing a face...or a landscape...a hundred times over and scatter the results everywhere. Birdhouses are built and hammered on posts outside. The birds come, lay eggs, and their lives join with ours.

There will be a day when the footsteps will fall silent. When the beds are made to perfection and the counter will stay clean for days on end.

I do not look forward to that day. I am content with reality right now.

Our lives may not be perfect, but they are well-lived.

Ironic Twist of Fate

Originally published on The Writings of A. K. Frailey 1/1/2019

In an ironic twist of fate, short-term memory loss has advantages. For example, it's great for my daily workout. I run downstairs on a specific errand...get sidetracked, drop the laundry into the dryer, sweep up a mess, and climb all the way to the top step before I realize that I really came down to get some frozen pumpkin to make a pie.

Short-term memory loss may also be one of the reasons mothers can enter into a third pregnancy as if they had never suffered morning sickness in their lives. Or why an otherwise perfectly sane person adopts a second puppy.

There are a lot of ways of peering at reality. Not that objective reality changes. Nooo. That's silly. Two plus two still adds up to four. Unless you want to throw in variables...or play socio-political mind games. But that's another story.

Still, I like to tell my kids that, as fate would have it, their weaknesses can, if utilized properly, become their greatest strength. Stubbornness heated in the fire of charity can be forged into loyalty. Unregulated passion can be shaped and molded into charity. Intellectual challenges can inform our human empathy. Physical imperfections can free us from societal-conformist chains.

When my daughter sliced her finger while making her very first batch of potato soup today, I kicked myself for not watching her more closely. But then I remembered that I learned to make potato soup pretty much the same way. The irony of injury is that we learn to be more careful, and potato soup eventually gets made without any unsavory ingredients.

My life appears to be stuffed with irony. The more I empty myself of selfish preoccupation, the more God widens the breadth and depth of my human journey. As I settle into the frozen stillness of winter, the more snugly the seeds of spring are embedded in my soul.

My memory loss doesn't seem to reach back to childhood, though. If anything, I can recall images and sensations more vividly as I grow older than ever before. Perhaps because in my mad rush to get pumpkin for pies and load washers and clean up messes, a part of me understands that every bit of this journey will become a memory. And as ironic reality would have...I might enjoy the moment more...then.

What Are We Searching For?
Originally published on The Writings of A. K. Frailey 1/9/2019

I decided to check the final stats on my blog this week. Nearly gave myself a heart attack. Not that it was bad...but the reality of the numbers and the fact that the globe was almost completely covered overwhelmed me. 65 countries have logged into my website this year, many of them multiple times. Even hundreds of times. The U.S., of course, topped the list with over 4000 views.

I'm from a generation where globetrotting was considered unusual. Travel abroad was for those with money and means. Granted, I grew up in a house where foreign students boarded with us from all over, so I understood the multicultural reality of our planet.

But websites and blogging have tightened the embrace.

On a given day, I may interact with people from half a dozen countries. And I might not even realize it. I'm used to calling my dad and asking about the weather in Kansas, but it still feels weird to ask a friend what the weather is like today in India. Or to be checking world time zones to see if someone would be available for a chat. And to consider that normal.

My kids play online games with people from all over the globe. But they don't see it as unusual. They've grown up with it. They may not be multilingual except for high school level Spanish or German, but they manage to make headway in a world dominated by computer technology.

Back in the day, science fiction was really fiction. Nowadays, we have nearly everything Captain Kirk had—but better. Granted, we don't travel to distant galaxies...or do we? We're building telescopes that can reach the edge of the universe. That's a pretty big reach.

We're exploring planets, stars, black holes, and outer space like never before in human history.

At the same time, we're discovering more about our universe on the opposite end of the spectrum. Go small and discover a whole new world. Look inside and travel deep into the microstructure of life.

It isn't just that we are interconnected, but we're a world changing at super speed at the same time. If Adam and Eve chomped on an apple for knowledge...I'd say we must be getting pretty close to the core.

Or maybe not.

God is infinite. Our search may go on forever.

Which begs the question: What are we searching for?

I remember returning to the U.S. from the Peace Corps in the Philippines and realizing that there was a lot of work that needed to be done in my own hometown. In my own family. I hardly needed to go across the planet to find a cause to live for, a love to die for, or a purpose to give meaning to my day.

I'm glad that my website reaches so many countries, and I'm glad that my kids are living in such illuminating times. But I can't help but wonder if we tend to look up when we should also look in. We're peering at a screen when we should be gazing into a pair of eyes.

Am I tapping a pad when I might be holding a hand?

Yes, I reached around the globe this past year, but have I touched a heart today?

Maybe I should tighten the embrace...indeed.

Brave Smile
Originally published on The Writings of A. K. Frailey 1/15/2019

I met a brave smile yesterday, and my faith in humanity flickered back to life. I had recently met with a painful disappointment, and I believed that a piece of my heart was broken beyond repair.

But I discovered that even a broken heart responds to a brave smile.

At the time, I was sitting between two young women I hardly knew, making light conversation with a few heavy topics thrown in for variety. The woman on my left was as innocent as the dawn of creation, but the one on my right smiled through sad eyes. Perhaps I read more than was there...perhaps I saw myself reflected in her gaze. But that was what amazed me. I dared to care.

As I drove home from Mass tonight, a storm flickered in the northern sky. There isn't usually lightning this time of the year, but the weather has been oddly mixed up. Probably just matching humanity's mood swings. From the CD player, a violin rose and fell in wild cadences, and on the horizon, clouds loomed like mountains. I drove through the black night with rustling trees swaying and dried corn stalks swirling from the barren fields like remnants of ghosts.

At Mass, Father had mentioned that life expectancy in the U.S. has dropped in the last few years, partially because of "diseases of despair"—addictions and suicide. This reality struck me as especially terrible in a generation with more technological and medical advancements and greater wealth, education, and entertainment opportunities than ever before. I guess the old saying is true: You can't buy happiness...or even a ray of hope. Later, as the priest held up the Host, I more clearly understood the reality of a perfect God coming as food to a starving and imperfect human race.

And loving us anyway.

I rarely know the deep grief of those around me, but I still find it comforting to remember when a young woman with sad eyes smiled at me.

The wind blows, rattling the windows as the threatening storm arrives, bringing freezing temperatures. Soon, the kids and I will watch part four of a series on John Quincy Adams, and I'll be reminded once again that humanity has faced mighty trials, both personal and societal, yet lived to tell the tale...despite our hurts and broken hearts.

Despair is not the only option to pain, grief, and fear. Courage and endurance are still possible. No doubt, you, too, have known your share of grief. Just a quick scroll through any social media platform or the news of the day is enough to make a person want to crawl under a rock. Forever.

But a brave smile offered me encouragement and solace when I needed it. I doubt she'll ever know. But you and I know.

A brave smile can enkindle a spark of hope in a world that needs it badly. Even if your heart is breaking...smile anyway.

Dare to care.

Looking On the Bright Side
Originally published on The Writings of A. K. Frailey 1/22/2019

I was trained as an election judge at the county courthouse, and I learned way more about elections than I ever thought I would. What astonished me were not the rules to keep track of the ballots, the attention to every detail in order to protect the voting process, but rather the people in the room with me. For the most part, my co-trainees had been doing this duty for years. Faithful and reliable. Exceptional really. It was humbling to realize—for the umpteenth time—how much I have taken for granted in my life.

Driving to get chicken for the kids' dinner—since I was way behind schedule and frankly fried chicken sounded really good at that point—I considered the cleared fields, the cars, and trucks rolling along the paved roads, the neat houses and yards, the orderly marketplace and quiet town, and I marveled at how much goes right in this world.

There is such a daily barrage of bad news that sometimes I feel inundated with the horrors of our human journey. But when I stop and look around, I can see that quite a few things actually go right each day.

Is it a matter of looking on the bright side? A Polly Anna disposition and all that? Perhaps not. Perhaps it is really assessing reality as it actually is. In fact, much of our world does run quite well by the hard work, decency, and generosity of a great number of people.

I've heard it said that the devil in hell doesn't buy a soul for a fortune—he only needs to offer trinkets. Well, I suspect that we sell our good humor, our cheerful dispositions, our positive outlook, our health, welfare, and even our sanity to the negative details of a world that can't possibly be perfect. How willing am I on an average day to gripe about a hundred things that aren't right, when I could just as easily thank God for a million things that have kept me alive and in decent shape?

The saleslady at the Walmart grumbled when I asked for three containers of chicken. She snarled at her co-worker. "Just put out a new batch, and she's clearing me out!"

Yikes! Guilty as charged. But the other woman winked at me and grinned with good humor. Guess which face I'm going to remember as I head home smiling...

Yep.

In the Souls of Those I Love
Originally published on The Writings of A. K. Frailey 1/29/2019

Since half my class was sick today, I decided to finish school early and do the next best thing—clean house. A good meal and a cup of hot tea were about the only offerings that made any sense to sick kids, but disinfectant, a broom, and a mop brought peace to my soul.

As I worked through the house, bottom to top, de-cluttering as I went, I considered the reality of humble duty and the rightness of simple actions well done. It's been said a thousand times that loving the little things makes for a quality life. And that was as true today as ever. But as the sun rose, peaked, and finally set, I sensed a release from the usual routine rush in my attention to minor details.

Like a child, I noticed each action almost as if it were in slow motion. Perhaps I was just tired. Perhaps I was in a state of grace. I became drawn away from the madness of the daily grind and the need to hurry through whatever toward a consideration of the people that I love. Smeared windows, mud on the floor, spills on the counter, crumbs across the table, dust everywhere, illness, and cranky moods are temporary. But each soul is unique and eternal, in growth—changing and developing—but alive beyond the lifetime of the stars.

As I sit here now and peer across a neat and tidy room, the lamp lit against the night sky, the fire crackling, my bookshelves straight, each pillow in its place, I admire the effect and the beauty of the moment. I also appreciate the quietness of kids in restful slumber, even the hamster as it runs on its wheel. Though I know that the dust will return and something will likely spill tomorrow, the beauty of this day will never be lost.

Laughter, smiles, conversation, kind deeds, and a gentle kiss will mark this day in its eternal place in history and in the souls of those I love.

Go Get 'Em, Girl
Originally published on The Writings of A. K. Frailey 2/5/2019

So, okay...I decided I'd had enough of the broken plastic tiles in the basement, and I was going to fix the problem once and for all. Go get 'em, girl!

I strode into the flooring store, ready to pick out a solution and get on with my life.

I entered said store and was immediately overwhelmed by the glorious selections hanging from wall to wall. I never realized I had been floor-deprived before, but I suddenly felt like I had entered a new dimension. One where floors stay politely underfoot and don't slide backward as you go out the door. Or fall to pieces if one dares to sweep out the corners.

A nice gentleman strode up and asked me a simple question, which quickly made me realize that I not only was I floor deficient; but I also have an uncanny ability to become an instant idiot. Recipe? Just ask a question and wait.

"So what are you looking for?"

Seemed like a straightforward query, but my one-word answer "flooring" didn't take us anywhere. I finally clued into his pointed stare and responded with "for a hallway and a bathroom," regaining a semblance of composure.

Which I lost again within seconds.

"So, what are the dimensions?"

He might as well have asked the circumference of the moon. I had realized approximately a nanosecond before he spoke—not only what he was going to ask—but that I had not a centimeter's clue as to the answer.

My I-might-as-well-fake-it response, "Well, about from here to the door and about yay-wide," only brought a completely composed expression from the salesman. Though I do suspect that behind the mask, he was wondering why he hadn't retired the day before.

Ladies, I feel I owe you a collective apology. Not only do I *never* knock out the bad guys like in every Marvel movie ever, but my retorts to clear questions are lame, and when face to face with the average salesman/repairman, I usually leave the impression that I don't know which end of a hammer pounds a nail.

Why is that?

It's not that I don't have any savvy role models in my life. I know plenty of intelligent, quick-witted women who can make conversation sparkle like champagne. But put me in a room with more than one other person—or a repair guy—and I might as well have been born in the Neolithic age.

Good Heavens! I've raised eight kids and lived to tell about it. My whole life is one escapade after another. But my adventures are not the big screen kind. And that may be part of my problem. Being a woman in the modern age appears to require a level of heroism unmatched in human history. And frankly, I don't know how the gorgeous, snappy-talking, totally composed, strong-as-titanium women presented to the world through big and little screens actually feel, but I wonder if the load gets a bit heavy sometimes.

I'm hardly advocating floor-dimension-ignorance when shopping for tiles, but I imagine that the sales guy wasn't nearly as scandalized by my imperfections as I was. I'll still tackle my list of home improvement projects, and hopefully, remember to bring any significant information into the process, but I won't bother to go into it with a kick-a attitude.

Too exhausting.

I will measure the floor, though.

I May Never Know Why
Originally published on The Writings of A. K. Frailey 2/7/2019

I had known Elaine all my life. Like a sister I never had. Yet I could not make it to her funeral. I couldn't. Perhaps I simply wouldn't. She had died long ago…

Growing up on the East Side, we knew we had it made. Life was good. Part-time jobs were easy to come by, school was never a serious challenge, and there was always tennis, soccer, or long walks by the lake.

I first started to notice a change when we were playing a game of tennis. She was always competitive, but this time, a missed shot didn't just spark irritation, it sparked rage. A repair guy on the roof nearby chuckled when she threw her racket. He sounded like the voice of God coming from a blue sky, "Shouldn't lose your temper like that, girl." Elaine looked like she'd heard a ghost, and I pretended not to know what she was talking about when she asked if I heard the voice. I just laughed.

But she didn't. She looked scared.

Throwing a racket was a little out of her normal emotional range, but fear, real fear, took her to a new universe.

I ignored the symptoms. I didn't think they were symptoms. I thought she was just being silly.

Before I knew what was happening, she was off to France to study for a semester. No big deal. I had plenty of studying at home to do. College and work-study kept me out of trouble. Well, for the most part.

But when she came home…something had changed. Her confidence had been shaken. It reminded me of another trip she'd taken the year before on some island or another. She had tried to explain about the people, their lifestyles…how different everything was… But I couldn't imagine. I didn't want to. Sounded pagan and vaguely selfish. Not a world I wanted to explore.

By the time she entered graduate school, she seemed bent on exploring extremes. If someone was having a wild time, she wanted in on it. No matter what that entailed. The wilder, the better.

I plodded through my courses and kept an eye on her. But I could not follow where she was going.

One day we walked along the lakeshore, and she explained ever so seriously that she was seeking help for depression. I shook my head. She had not the slightest reason to be depressed. She had a good family, an excellent education, she had traveled far and wide, and she had a wonderful future...if only she would see it.

But she couldn't see it. She couldn't feel it. A friend of hers had committed suicide the month before, and it weighed on her mind. She was afraid it would spread like cancer. She'd be next.

I told her to shut up and quit thinking like that.

Elaine pleaded with me, stomping along like a little girl. "I need help. I'm sick...on the inside. Medication might help."

I remember feeling so old. Worldly wise in my vast years of watching family members destroy themselves with drug and alcohol cure-alls. I grabbed her arm and glared into her eyes. "Medication can't help you. Tough this out. Once you're on that stuff...you'll never get off it."

She pulled away, dragging her fingers through her short hair the way she always did. "You can't understand. I'm mentally ill. I'm crazy."

I laughed. "By the very fact that you know you're crazy means that you're not really crazy. In pain. Yes. Upset. Of course. But you can work this out...give yourself time. Not drugs."

I might as well have been talking to the trees.

Before I knew what was happening, she was on an anti-depressant regime that would have knocked a rhino off its feet. It seemed to work. She finished graduate school without major problems...except for a map-laminating incident.

Then she went to look for work and torpedoed nearly every offer she got.

I took a job in another city and shut my eyes to her issues, hoping they'd just go away. Hoping she'd grow strong again.

She called me one day from a state out west. She was visiting family and thought she had accidentally taken her medication twice...enough to kill her. I told her to go see a doctor. She hung up.

By the time she called again, I was married, had three kids, and she was engaged. We agreed to meet up in our old hometown first chance we got. When we did run into each other months later, she looked very much like the girl who threw her racket across the court. But she smiled when she hugged my kids.

I sighed in relief. Time can heal even the most wounded souls. Even souls that should not be wounded at all. Even souls that appear to wound themselves.

Or so I thought.

The next call I got was from her brother. She had been killed crossing a street. She had stepped in front of a truck.

He wanted to know if I would fly out for the funeral. I was nursing my infant, and it was the middle of winter...I had a lot of reasons not to go.

But I doubt I would've gone even if her casket was next door and springtime flowers fluttered in the breeze.

Little by little, Elaine had died. Not from childhood trauma, or teen rebellion, or even cultural clashes. Somewhere along the line, her sanity, her identity and her will to live a healthy life had eroded until there was only a thread left. And one day, that thread snapped.

I may never know why.

A lot of years have passed...and I've never stopped praying for her. For the truth of it is, I now realize, she never really died.

Elaine will always live in spirit...and in me.

To believe in god
Originally published on The Writings of A. K. Frailey 2/12/2019

I took a couple of the kids to the Christian Mission Thrift Store this week. We usually drop some stuff off, and if the kids see something in their price range that they like, blessings follow.

As they wandered down the knick-knack racks (say that five times fast), I wandered over to the brick "prayer wall" where people post prayer intentions. Contemporary Christian music played in the background—a rather good beat, I might add.

I stood there and read the Post-it notes...one after another. I wasn't surprised by the "Please pray for my...who has cancer." Or the "Prayers for my friend, injured in a car accident." Or any of them...until I came to the very last note centered at the bottom and scrawled slantwise across the paper: "...to believe in god."

Neat small letters.

My heart nearly broke.

I'm not entirely sure why this note filled my eyes with tears. But it did. Such an honest plea.

Terrible things happen, and humanity is stuck with the default reality that we will suffer and die at some point on this journey. But when a person believes in God, there is hope...the possibility of joy that can transcend all suffering and even death itself.

But if you don't believe in God...or even god...you find yourself at the mercy of fate and all the little hells of human existence.

Though I have questioned why certain things have happened in my life, I've rarely—even for a moment—doubted the existence of God. He is as real to me as my own skin. The only times I've doubted His supernatural existence is when I have placed Him on my human level and discovered I really don't see Him as clearly as I want to.

Lesson #1—God is God, and I am not.

My faith is a pure gift. I don't deserve it. I never earned it. And I grieve for those who don't share it.

As I drove the kids home with their newfound treasures—gifts I know they plan on giving for the next birthday or holiday—I am grateful not only for my faith but also for the anonymous note on that brick wall.

To pray for faith...is the beginning.

God will do the rest.

A Timeless Truth
Originally published on The Writings of A. K. Frailey 2/19/2019

Henrietta has escaped, and my daughter is dearly worried. Henrietta has been missing all day. Henrietta is a hamster.

The truth is, I heard Henrietta scrabbling at her cage, saw that it was two in the morning, mumbled, "No bloody way," and pulled the covers over my head to keep out the cold. And any furry visitors.

My daughter got up, comforted her progeny, and went back to bed.

But did that satisfy the quadruped? Nope. Henrietta chewed a hole through a cage any decent rodent would be proud of and ran off to golly-knows-where.

As my kids searched the house from top to bottom, I tried really hard to get emotionally invested. I squinted so I could remember what the tan and white critter looked like, squeezed my heart into kid-remembrances of former rodent pets, cajoled my mood to get into the spirit of concern...but...frankly, it was a losing battle.

I've had too many episodes with mice in the cabinets, rats in the outbuildings, possums in the feed sacks, and countless other run-ins with wildlife to get overly upset over a missing hamster.

But that doesn't mean I don't care about Henrietta. I do care, for one very good reason: My daughter cares.

There have been many instances in my life where I have had to stretch my emotional bank account into new territory. Many the time, I have stood before an array of photos while family members gushed through wonderful memories, smiling, giggling, outright belly laughing at memories of so-and-so doing such-and-such and nudging me in the ribs as if I shared their glorious past. I had no clue. No memory. No warm feelings. No shared gush of any kind.

I learned after one particularly dramatic episode when a friend laughed till she nearly cried to look—not at the photo—but rather at the person remembering. The one still loving. Then I discovered that I could join in. Sort of.

In some weird, mysterious way, I could then see the baby, the brother, the husband, or the mother through familiar eyes and gain a semblance of the reality they were seeing. I never actually co-opted their memories. I could never go back in time and experience those exact memories of nights rocking the little one, sibling pillow fights, intimate spousal lovemaking, or parental forgiveness, but I could love the person standing next to me as they remembered. That act of love crosses time, distance, and even death itself. The remembered loved one might as well have been perched on the arm of the couch, filling in the details. They become that real.

So now, when photos are pulled out, I don't pull away. I look, listen, and watch the walls of reality open to a timeless truth. Sincere love does not die. It may lie quietly on a shelf for years but pull out the photos…and it lives once again.

As for Henrietta, she must have been sleeping. Once night fell, her tummy awoke, and she sashayed into the middle of the bedroom looking for all the world as if she owned the place and expected room service. My daughter scooped her up, offered a minor scold, fed, and played with her. Lucky rodent.

Okay, the truth is, I don't feel any closer to Henrietta…but I still care. Because love can be shared. Even with a hamster.

Supernatural Synchronization
Originally published on The Writings of A. K. Frailey 3/5/2019

Today I sat in the car waiting for kid #8 to finish her piano lesson while a CD daughter #1 put together with a variety of music played in the background. I finished saying the Rosary, and then I watched the wind run rampant over the yard, tugging at ribbons tied to posts, and setting tree branches dancing. A strange synchronization of music and rippling grass made me sit up and take notice.

I've been reading Christopher West's book *Theology of the Body*, which delves into the mysteries of the human experience as body and soul and God's manifestations of love through His desire to unite with us. The concept of "Spiritual Communion" in terms of the human race, past, present, and future is familiar to me, so I wasn't completely overwhelmed by the profound sense of unity I experienced as the wind and music swept over me.

What did raise my heart beat was when I started thinking about how this world is full of mysterious gateways and then the literal gate directly in front of me broke free from its constraint and bounced wide open. Now that startled me. But I had to smile.

As the music slowed and the song ended, a cloud swept overhead and darkened my little part of the world. At that same moment, the wind disappeared. All was quiet, dark, and still. My heart pounded a little harder.

When the next song started, the cloud vanished; sunbeams streaked across the ground, and the wind rose up and animated everything in its path. The glory of music and nature along with this supernatural harmony was impossible to miss.

I'm sure there are many explanations for the beauty of those moments. But as I drove my daughter home and reentered the "real" world, I didn't care about explanations. I felt as if I had encountered a moment of spiritual lovemaking, and I wasn't going to mess it up with words or rationales.

Sometimes, I suspect, the reason we humans get so lost and depressed isn't because no one knows or loves us. It's simply because we don't know ourselves, Whose we are, and accept the love that is staring us in the face.

I started out this morning convinced that I was a failure on a hundred levels. I sat in a car and allowed something mysterious to happen. I did not will it. I did not deserve it. But I sure did accept it.

I'm home now and there is no music and little wind, but my heart is still beating, and I'm smiling.

A New Heart
Originally published on The Writings of A. K. Frailey
3/26/2019

My dad turned ninety years old recently. That milestone made me think. I counted up how many of my friends or family are now in their nineties and the number surprised me. Almost two handfuls. And if I add in friends and family in their eighties, the number jumps much higher. Middle-aged friends make up the vast majority of people I know.

Most of these people are active, still drive, and have their wits about them. Yet they can't live forever, and I know that I'll be attending a lot of funerals in the future.

One thought led to another...

I don't see many pregnant women anymore. In fact, if I see a pregnant woman or a woman with an infant, I tend to feel surprised. Why? Because there are so few.

I did some checking and stopped counting after eight Google pages of recent reports stating that fertility rates have dropped drastically in the last few years. Though it didn't surprise me, it did send a chill up my spine when I remembered how old most of my friends are.

I find it troubling to think that in the most prosperous age in human development where we have the greatest labor savings devices, the best nutrition, the widest variety of entertainment, astonishing medical advancements, the largest food production ever...we also have a rising suicide rate and a declining fertility rate.

In our current world, we tout the glorious possibility of eliminating children and old people...Down Syndrome children, a baby with health issues, unwanted kids. We tell elderly folks that they don't have to live sad and depressed lives...they can kill themselves. Legally. And we'll call it progress.

But I wonder. Who are we killing?

Our nation is obsessed with political issues and social causes. We are a nation at war with itself and within itself. But we aren't an isolated nation anymore. If you haven't noticed—our problem is the world's problem. The world's problem is ours.

We're in trouble. But we can't seem to stop screaming at each other long enough to realize that the ship we, and our kids, are on is going down.

I don't have a family-therapy solution big enough to fit the whole world. Sure wish I did. But then, I'm not sure we need to fix the world. Perhaps...we just need to stop hating the people around us. Even the ones who disagree with us...the ones who drive us crazy with their policies. Hate won't plug our leaky boat.

I imagine that when Christ told the angels that He was going to become a man, they probably thought He was crazy. Stupid. Irrational. After all, God had angels! What did He need with a bunch of corporeal beings trapped in time with limited intelligence?

So, I suspect that the cosmic break wasn't over belief in God...it was over belief in human beings. After all, the devil knows who God is. But what He doesn't know...is who we are. Who we are called to become...

Nope. The devil is pretty sure we are disgusting beasts who can't be trusted with anything important.

Question is...who do *we* think we are?

If we continue to hate each other and kill our children, our elders, and ourselves...the answer is a sad one indeed.

Perhaps we need more than a change of perspective. Perhaps we need a new heart.

One that doesn't kill.

A Better Point
Originally published on The Writings of A. K. Frailey 4/2/2019

It was supposed to be a fairly simple day. Teach school. Take kids to piano lessons. Go shopping. Try to balance the bank account. Life in all its humdrum reality. Except it wasn't. Practically never is in my world.

Last week I had similar plans on Tuesday, but instead, I got a call from daughter number one telling me that her car sat dead as a doornail in the university parking lot. After a great deal of running around, which by sheer chance included towing said dead car to a service station I knew and loved that happened to be closed, and therefore towing it to another service station, I managed to pick up my daughter after her late class at the university.

As we're driving along a windy country road in the black of night with only a few iridescent eyes staring at us from the roadside (and one near collision with a bunny) I turned on a CD that my daughter had made for me. I was just about to skip a French song (I secretly didn't like) when she informed me that it was her favorite. Huh?

Soooo, I played the song, and as I drove around curves and ignored the roadside glares, she translated the words and explained the singer's life history. Not only did I gain a new appreciation for French music, but I gained fresh insight into my daughter's mind and soul. Well worth the price of a car battery and a tow.

Now this Tuesday, second daughter's car battery lay down and died conveniently in my driveway. But since she had an exam and lab work, I offered her my car and before you could say, "Whoa there!" she also had my phone tucked in her purse. Yep, happy to oblige.

Well, I was...until I found myself circling our church building, trying to find a legal way into the House of God. Daughter number three had music lessons, and I wasn't about to let her down. If only I had a cell phone to let the teacher know. But, alas!

So I squared my shoulders and trooped to the legal office across the street and asked to borrow their phone for a quick call...or five as it turned out. They were amazingly gracious. As if phoneless, harassed mothers walked in every day begging telephone assistance.

It wasn't until I climbed into bed that I realized that from one week to the next I had asked the assistance of at least half a dozen people, and every single one of them had responded with generosity and kindness. I had also learned the meaning of a French song, the sad life history of a singer, seen the inside of an office I had long wondered about and trusted that, most likely everything would work out just fine. And it had.

Perhaps a simple life isn't the point. Perhaps just living life as it comes with dead batteries, iridescent eyes, locked doors, missing phones, and the need for help makes a better point. Simple or complicated—live.

Learn As I Go
Originally published on The Writings of A. K. Frailey 4/16/2019

I was sitting in the doctor's office, and a mother came in with the world's cutest toddler. This child could have ousted Shirley Temple off the stage for sheer adorableness. It wasn't just the white bow wrapped around her head, her moccasin slippers, or her bright blue eyes...it was her bubbling enthusiasm for everything and everyone in the room. She was absolutely certain that the world was a wonderful place, and everyone was her best friend.

As I watched the mini bundle of energy scamper to the nearest toy, her mother followed close behind, her hands at the ready for any slips or trips. Soon, mom had her little one ensconced in her lap and helped her baby push the colored beads along the complex wire arrangement that probably made some toy maker rich.

In my lap, I gripped my latest to-do list. Among all the usual tasks of the week, I had outlined jobs and assignments for each of my kids. Since my children have an age range from 23 to 10, I have to consider their abilities in relation to their experience and natural inclinations. A kid who loves animals to distraction is better at remembering to feed the dogs and cats than a kid who would rather spend the morning reviewing Italian cuisine recipes.

Over the years, I have altered and re-altered my mothering techniques to the point where I am very reluctant to tell another mom how to do it right. I vividly recall a couple that presented to my husband and me their most successful child-rearing philosophy—"Use common sense." Right. Sounds great. But what does that mean when facing a screaming baby whose diaper is dry and tummy is full, a toddler with a purple ring around his mouth who can't seem to remember what he ate to get the vibrant hue on his face, a little girl who has packed her bag to go to boarding school without telling mom a thing about it, a son who asks what to do with his life, or grieved kids when they discover that not only is life not fair, but human beings can be vicious without cause.

Being a parent is a little like being God. But without the power and the glory. For a time, a parent has a say about everything. To the point of utter exhaustion. But little by little, that power erodes, as well it must, and the child grows into his own decision-making being. Then, the parent must step out of the way. The child must lead.

But what about when they don't see the need? What if mom or dad have been so good at what they do and the world so darn comfortable, that it is simply easier to continue in the comfort zone? Truth be told, it's no fun getting out of the perfect-parent zone, either. It's peaceful and enjoyable to hold a baby in your lap and move their hand, as you know how it should go for the best effect.

As I consider our world today, I think of all our comfort zones. A world where so much is given to us. Where our feet are directed to schools. Our minds are directed in classes. Our passions are directed through media. Our faith is directed through traditions and habits. I have to wonder, when does direction become strangulation?

The cute baby I saw today charmed everyone in the waiting room. In the best scenario, she'll grow up and better the world through her chosen passions and abilities. But to get to that point, she'll have to sit by herself, and mom will have to let go of her hand.

I don't have a quick formula for parenting. Like my kids, I learn as I go. But the key is—learn to let go. We have to allow our kids to grow up and make their own choices and face real-life consequences.

Though we're never far behind.

For even if our hands don't touch, surely our hearts do.

Another Season
Originally published on The Writings of A. K. Frailey 4/30/2019

I took up an old pail, a sponge, and cleanser and scrubbed up the old chick pen this morning. The sun shone, and birds chirped to the glory of springtime. After the long, frozen winter, freedom from thick sweaters and heavy coats felt like being released from prison. Dirt, dead spiders, and unmentionables fell away from the wood as I scrubbed foamy detergent over the rough surface. It took a couple of rounds, scrubbing, rinsing, and scrubbing again before I found the pure white paint under all the accumulated grit and goo.

Though I wasn't exactly getting cleaner as I continued the process, I did identify with the sensation of dropping old cares and worn-out worries. As warmer weather arrives with its windy arms out like a long-lost relative, boots, coats, gloves, and all the assorted outerwear can be washed, sorted, and put away. The woodstove can be cleaned one last time and shut down for the season. My kids will finish their final tests, close their books, and head outside like soldiers returning from a long campaign in the trenches. The animals will shed their winter coats, and new grass will spring up through the brown and lifeless stems of last fall. Birds are nesting, and frogs have already assembled on the brink of the pond like a church choir, ready to croak their hearts out.

I tend to think of autumn and winter as the contemplative seasons of the year, but that is not necessarily so. In the turning of each season, there is a process of ending before the new beginning.

I watched a new mother proudly showing off her new baby the other day. I could feel her exultation. In the early days, I'd hear stories of mothers sending their kids off to college...or planning weddings...or welcoming grandchildren...and I couldn't comprehend their joy. I could only identify with the new mother.

But now I've lived through enough parental stages that I can join the proud mother's moment, sigh in relief at a graduation, grin at a kid's first paycheck, and know that in time, the rest will come.

I can also grieve in lost innocence and cry in shared pain. Sometimes, winter storms break branches and tear whole trees from the yard. Sometimes, the power goes out, and it seems like it will never come back on again. Sometimes, loved ones get sick—or old—and they pass from the current of our lives. At times, selfish weakness rears its ugly head, and innocent souls suffer. In the worst of dark winter, the cold seeps from the blustery outdoors into the marrow of my bones, and I wonder if I even want to see another season.

But despite wintertime sorrows, eventually, light breaks through the clouds, warmth revitalizes my skin, and, as the gleaming white pens soak up the brilliant sunshine and spring buds burst from the tips of trees, I can respectfully put away the worn-out season. I'll pack it neatly away where it belongs and let it rest. After all, each turn of the year, like a chapter in life's book, is unique and precious, deserving a gracious goodbye before facing the future with a hopeful hello.

Along the Roadside
Originally published on The Writings of A. K. Frailey 5/7/2019

Early this spring, I was taking my usual walk, and I couldn't help but notice three beer cans in my path. Annoyed, I picked them up. And then I picked up an empty whiskey flask, a crushed cigarette pack, and a slimy soda bottle... By the time I made it home, I had an armload, and I really needed a shower and a change of clothes.

So then began a weekly stroll farther and farther along the roadside, picking up whatever garbage caught my eye. Yesterday, I completely ignored the fact that it was windy and that we had had a rainstorm the night before. I sauntered out with three trash bags in hand. What can I say? It was sunny, and I was feeling ambitious.

Pumped with the sensation that I could at least do this little thing well, I began to pick up bottles, cans, broken car pieces—though I was momentarily stumped when I came to a hubcap and a bumper—I couldn't fit those into my bags.

Cars passed, and at first, I'd look up and wave. Occasionally I could see the face of the person driving. Clearly, they weren't sharing my joy. On the contrary, they looked either concerned or bewildered.

As I shuffled along and my bags got heavier, I pondered the situation. I tried to see what I looked like from a driver's perspective. Then it hit me. I could easily be mistaken for a vagrant, someone doing community service for a traffic violation, or a disgruntled do-gooder. After all, my wave and smile had disappeared after the first quarter mile.

By the time I reached the edge of town, I knew I had to turn back. Actually, common sense would've had me turn back a half-mile ago, but picking up bottles and cans can be amazingly addictive. It's like finding another prize to add to your collection. You just have to ignore the fact that your toes are squishing in muck, and your hands don't smell so good anymore.

A neighbor stopped on my return trip and offered to take the bags in his truck, and I, like the complete idiot I can sometimes be, waved him off. I thought I could just finish the north side of the road, and besides, home wasn't that far away.

Yeah. Right.

Did I mention that heavy rain can turn fields into sucking quicksand, and strong winds over an open field are nothing to sniff at? Well, once my bags were full to the bursting point, turns out that they also equal the weight of a bloated elephant. And lo and behold, I was carrying three bulging sacks, creating a wall that just demanded to be knocked down.

Yeah, yeah, yeah, I made it home and sorted the cans and plastics, and I even took them to the recycling center. But as I pondered my aching shoulders today, I had to consider why this whole scenario seemed so bizarrely familiar.

How many times in life have I tried to pick up the trash along the roadside of life, and, in the process, got a few weird stares and a bit messy? Did I mention aching arms?

It seems that following an inspiration to do some small good in the world does not necessarily equate with enjoying the sensation beyond the first few moments of self-satisfied pleasure. More often than not, I have found that following up on a good deed involves all sorts of complications and grimy realities I never considered at the outset.

If I listen to my shoulders, I'll never take a trash bag down the road again. But then, as I returned home from the recycling center, a beer can lay there, sprawled on the ground like an intoxicated groundhog, and I knew I'd be back.

After all, it was the only one...

Love Anyway
Originally published on The Writings of A. K. Frailey 5/21/2019

I've never been particularly good with suffering. Avoidance? Insecurity? Hyper-control? Sure. Then my all-star qualities shine bright. But being insecure, hyper-controlling, and trying to avoid pain doesn't a happy life make.

When I was twenty-one, I had the chance to meet my father after long years of separation at—of all places—the Art Institute of Chicago. I was meeting his second wife for the first time. And to make matters even more relaxed, I didn't know a thing about modern art. But I did discover a latent sense of humor, which apparently shot to the surface like a geyser when under serious pressure.

I amused my dad, his wife, and even myself. Seeing absurdities in the uncomfortable world before me kept my eyes averted from haunting ghosts and garrulous gremlins. Our conversation never veered toward my mom, my brothers or sisters, loss of childhood, alcoholism, substance abuse, or neglect. The conversation stayed right where it needed to be, focused on pictures hanging on walls, which none of us understood.

Contrary to every psychological theory I knew at the time, communication was not the key to our relationship. After that initial reunion, I visited my dad regularly. He attended my wedding, got to know my growing family, and became a steady fixture in my life. Even at the age of ninety, we still connect at least once a week. He may not remember my name some days, but he always remembers that he loves me. And that I love him.

Over the years, we did have a couple of hard conversations about our family and the things that went so very wrong in our lives, but they were not all that productive. His simple admission, "I'm sorry," was all I ever really needed to hear. And my, "I love you anyway," was all he really needed to know.

In recent years, I have lost a husband, a brother, several friends (I have a visitation to attend this weekend), my sense of worth, and even my heart, but in experiencing these losses, I have discovered that there is no fixing pain. There is only, "I'm sorry." And "I love you anyway."

Being truly sorry when someone is suffering shares the burden. It is one of the greatest acts of generosity that a human being can undertake.

Loving anyway explodes the walls of control, doubt, fear, hurt, avoidance, and insecurity. Love is not doormat material. Love demands decency, honesty, integrity, and heroism. But it doesn't demand those qualities all at once in perfect order.

After a particularly brutal loss recently, my imagination conjured up the image of a wounded woman rising after tumbling down a hill. Not unlike Sam at the base of Mount Doom. How's that for an "I'm sorry, and I love you anyway" scenario? But Sam rose again. Even when it was hopeless to do so. Even when pain had the upper hand. Even at the end of Middle-earth, he rose and loved anyway. And he wasn't alone.

Pain and loss are twin hells that human beings experience in umpteen versions throughout the course of our journey toward heaven. We can't fix reality, stop the hurt, make everything right, control outcomes, or even avoid tumbling down hills. Personally, I can crack a joke and laugh at absurdities to keep the ghosts and gremlins at bay, and that helps. Some.

But mostly, I can be sorry and love anyway.

Whispering In My Ear
Originally published on The Writings of A. K. Frailey 5/28/2019

There is no end to the reproductive abilities of my to-do list. As soon as I send half a dozen items into obliteration, it squares its shoulders, huffs like an angry rhino, and spontaneously combusts fourteen new items for me to get done before the end of the week. I can hear them pop into existence all the way from the kitchen.

So this week, after I whittled my list down to a mere four items, I decided to play a trick on my merciless taskmaster; I drove to the lake and stared over the rippling waves, where no list could follow. The sound of the wind would surely block any distant popping.

And you know, it worked. For a while.

Unfortunately, that did not stop my brain from working overtime. As I soaked up the warm sun and my skin prickled under the influence of a cool wind, I noted that life is full of inexplicable ironies.

For example, we got our chicks nicely ensconced in their outdoor pen. Two of my children are their primary guardians during their growing season. After approximately seven weeks, the chicks go from adorable hopping balls of yellow fluff to ugly *Gallus gallus domesticus.* (I kid you not—that's their scientific name—ask Google.) And astonishingly soon, they are the main course at dinner.

How is it possible that on one day, I feel protective of the little featherheads, and in a short time, I'm...well...you know? Basically, the answer has a lot to do with the fact that chicks grow into chickens. And my family needs to eat.

Consider the more challenging irony of being born to die, loving people even when it hurts like hell, how good intentions can go so very wrong, and a host of other questionable realities. I may have silenced my main taskmaster, but life is never done whispering in my ear.

This morning, my to-do list sent me to the Salvation Army, but it took a deep longing to steer my car to the lake, a full heart to soak in the warm sunshine, and a grateful mind to accept the temperate breeze. As I stared at the waves, time slowed, birds screamed at each other, and I smiled at their antics. Eventually, God and I conversed, though I did most of the talking. And all the while, the Earth continued to spin on its axis, and all of humanity lived their lives without me.

But by the time the sun started its downward journey, my stomach was rumbling, a faint pop sounded in the distance, and life—with all its ironies and perplexities—called to me.

I'm home now, and the chicks are running about their pen like the carefree *Gallus gallus domesticus* they are. The sun is still shining, and the breeze is stronger than ever. I'm still talking, and God is still listening. And my to-do list can reproduce at will.

Living Spring Time
Originally published on The Writings of A. K. Frailey 6/4/2019

The school year is over, the last recital is done, and springtime is in full swing. The trees have blossomed and are leafed out, bees buzz from flower to flower, frogs croak in the creek, coyotes sing their chorus, and anonymous owls freak me out with their various shrieks in the dead of night. It's a sublime time of the year. Everything is bursting with new life.

Almost everything.

My elderly friend and fellow Fillmorian, Wilda, passed away a few days ago, and my heart aches. It's not that she wasn't well cared for or that no one loved her. She was loved and cared for. But when I last visited her...it was a series of painful goodbyes. I miss my friend.

Our mutual friend, Margaret, died last month. Our Afternoon Ladies' Teas with Wilda as advisor and organizer are over. The days when the kids could go to her house and do odd jobs, talking and chatting, asking questions, and keeping her company are gone.

When I sat with her the last time and held her hand in the nursing home, I wasn't depressed. I had a lump in my throat I could not swallow away and an ache burning my eyes, but I knew beyond all shadow of a doubt that we have been blessed to know each other. For this, I will always be grateful.

As I sat by her wheelchair the other day in the central room, someone turned on music, the kind from decades ago—a 40s tune—and suddenly, one of the old men started to sing. Powerfully. His head was back, his eyes were closed, and he was singing gloriously at the top of his lungs. My heart rose.

I looked around the circle; I knew there was at least one couple. Many were widows or widowers. Some had their eyes closed, but several joined in the song too.

I don't know about you, but for me, the 40s have always brought up images of the war years, devastation, and hard times. Trials and separations. Fear and loss.

Yet these elderly people had lived through all of that...and much more. And, now, in a nursing home, with music playing, songs warbling from myriad throats, and with their eyes closed, they had a brief respite. They were living their springtime again.

I have another friend, always cheerful, that I visit. Helen's pleasant, upbeat attitude never falters. She and her husband just celebrated their seventy-first anniversary. They lived together in that same nursing home for a time. Thank God, they are home now...my kids are able to help them manage through the week, so they have a different fate...one created by their children where they can stay at home in familiar surroundings, in the world they crafted through long years of love and hard work.

I've met a series of people recently who have told me about their baggage. Their divorces. Their mistakes. How they want to start over and try again. A new relationship. A new life. New hope. Springtime. Our hearts yearn for a new beginning. A chance to get beyond bad memories and live a new life. A better life.

But this one couple stands in testimony of the passage through the dark times. The light at the end. The hope that lives, not in the future, but as a committed ever-present now.

All my elderly friends have their lives bundled up in long years of experience. The good. The bad. Springtime warmth...and winter cold. Marriage and family relationships, like memories, are a collection of what was…and what is…not what-ifs. Love and friendship are a passionate embrace of a thousand daily realities, hanging in there and holding on.

So, now, I'm sitting on my back porch, staring at the new onions, potatoes, peppers, and tomato plants, the sounds of nature vibrating in my ears, and yet, I can hear that old man singing. I can see that elderly woman cutting up her husband's meat so he can eat his dinner. I can feel Wilda's hand in mine.

On Both Sides of the Road
Originally published on The Writings of A. K. Frailey 6/18/2019

I'm sitting on a green lawn amid leafy trees while on the road behind me, cars drive through a busy intersection, and a shopping mall bustles with mid-day shoppers. Occasionally, a horn blasts in the distance, informing some unfortunate driver that he or she has pushed another driver's patience to the limit.

In front of me, a solid series of stone buildings stand in testimony to an idea and an ideal that most people can hardly comprehend. The dedication of one's life to an unseen God.

Here stands a convent in the midst of a big city. An American flag flutters in the breeze. A statue of Mary hovers several feet above the ground in a wall niche. Crosses pierce the blue sky at the top of two buildings.

Since this convent caters to the needs of the elderly, several old women have been wheeled to cars in the parking lot. Family members (or friends) have taken loved ones out for the day to whatever adventure.

I sit here with my computer on a grassy lawn as flying insects pursue their destiny, occasionally bumping into my arm or landing on my keys, annoying me...perhaps being annoyed by me. I don't know. Though I sincerely hope not. Considering the fact that I just squashed one...

Nature in all forms seems to flourish amid the grassy lawn and the leafy trees: insects, birds, squirrels, trees, flowers, and humans of all ages and descriptions. The contrast of old world and new world, a supernatural reality inside and a natural reality outside hardly escapes my notice.

Crossing the road from a mall to a convent seems unlikely. But apparently, it's very doable. As I listen to the chirping of birds, I can see the boughs of trees where they nest. Each bird sings a particular song for its breed and builds a specific nest for its kind. They do not choose their songs or their nests. They are driven by an invisible force to sing...to nest...to live, and eventually to die in a cycle that has been rotating since the dawn of creation.

But the women in the convent chose to live here. They could have become doctors or builders, teachers, or songwriters. They could have lived in a big house in the city or a straw hut on an island. They could've joined The Peace Corps or taken up computer hacking as their chosen careers.

We all have certain paths before our feet...well-worn roads rutted with the footsteps of our parents, grandparents, and humdrum life experiences. But we set our path by what we decide to see and what we choose to ignore. What we respond to and what we jerk away from.

As a young woman, I visited with nuns many times, and I served as a teacher with sisters in a convent in Chicago. So the world of religious life is not foreign to me. It is simply not mine. I never felt called to that life. I can't say why any more than the birds can explain why a certain twig attracts their eye...or why worms seem yummy but chocolate leaves them cold.

Our life path may seem a mystery, but there is more to our choices than grandmother's alcoholic tendencies, Mom's DNA, dad's offer to take up the family business, the car accident that makes us wonder why we aren't all dead yet, or a hundred other realities. They inform us...but they aren't all that form us.

In a little while, I'll make the drive back through Missouri into Illinois, and if all goes well, arrive home safe and sound. My dogs will greet me. They might even lift their heads in acknowledgment of my existence. A couple cats will blink in my direction...at least one will demand a rubdown. Kids will say hi and ask how things went or when's dinner...

In time, the sun will set on a day when I celebrated Mass with women and girls who see possibilities that nature cannot speak about, but they witness in a way few humans dare. A day of trucks and cars, kids and animals, natural and supernatural realities.

The Holy Spirit goes where it will. It forms and informs us. Love is like that. So is joy.

But while a bird cannot choose its song, we can choose our joy. Circumstances may limit our universe, but we can choose what we focus on, what we respond to, and how we act.

Perhaps we want a twig, but we have only clay. We can choose to make something good from that clay. It may not look like any house we've ever seen before, but it can make a life, one with an outside and an inside. We can sing and build and live on both sides of the road.

The Real Reason
Originally published on The Writings of A. K. Frailey 6/25/2019

Last evening, I sat on the back porch and watched fireflies twinkle, appearing at different spots in our beautiful garden like Tolkien-esk-fairies. When I tipped my head back, I could see faint stars turning ever brighter as the blue sky darkened to dusky-purple.

The kids still living at home slumbered in their beds. The dogs and cats stretched out on the porch. The garden rested without chiding me for neglect. Peace and contentment pervaded my little universe, and my heartbeat slowed to the rhythm of a lovely universe.

Then a mosquito bit me. A moth fluttered close and attempted to smack me in the face.

What the—?

I decided I had tempted fate long enough, and I rose to my feet. I was just about to go inside when the phone rang. It was my daughter who had moved into her own place last week. With a lurch, my heart gripped the phone harder than my hand. It was so good to hear her voice. To chat. To know she was okay. Yeah, I had figured she was fine...but now I knew. Happiness. Even better than contentment.

Later, as I crawled into bed, a soft cool breeze rippled the curtains, sending a chill down my spine. I realized, for the umpteenth time, that I'm in a new period of adjustment. I can name four families without blinking that are going through the same adjustment—transitioning on a weekly, sometimes daily, basis from caring for aged parents to children flying from the nest.

Was there ever a time when life was simple? When the fireflies ruled, and the stars stayed still? If there was, it didn't last long.

One of the things I always loved about Tolkien's stories was the way he managed to include some kind of retreat. A time-out. Or maybe, a time-in. It was a period where the characters would get off the road, luxuriate in a hot bath, shift into clean clothes, eat honey and homemade bread, and enjoy a bit of peace and quiet.

I've been pregnant eleven times, lost a husband to cancer, and raised eight kids over twenty-three years. I could try and list the number of things in the house that I have fixed, but it would be a fake number since I usually have to fix the same blessed thing multiple times. I've supervised innumerable gardens, raised chickens, stacked woodpiles, managed accounts, planned and executed educational programs, and done whatever job/task/mission seemed necessary to ensure the health and wellbeing of my family...and my sanity.

Days run together like a stream joining the ocean. Yet, over time, the stream of life changes course. Challenges are met and new missions accepted. Chickenpox, the death of a beloved pet, toppled trees, a shoulder injury, a new electric appliance, a scholarship, college, a new job...

Being a child and loving our parents—difficult as that sometimes can be—seems easy when you become a parent yourself and look back—I had it easy then. Raising a baby seems heroic until you get to the teen years and wonder how the human race ever survived. Each new challenge seems to play a game of one-up-man-ship with the stage before.

So, that's why God created fireflies. And starry skies. The real reason behind hot showers and cool breezes. I'll never actually get to Tom Bombadil's house, but I can sit on the back porch, nibble a chocolate-zucchini-nut muffin, and watch the fireflies twinkle and the stars turn.

And answer the phone when it rings.

Take It Easy and Get Back to Work
Originally published on The Writings of A. K. Frailey 7/2/2019

I decided I needed a break. I'd take it easy for a week. Read a novel. Take afternoon naps. Enjoy leisurely strolls down the road. Really rest up.

By Sunday evening, I was depressed beyond words.

Turns out that my mind can only take so much perfection. Then I ache for a problem to solve. A kitchen to clean. A fly to swat.

Not to give the impression that the rest didn't do me good. But even a rest needs to end. There comes a point when "rest" becomes the newest line on the to-do list...except nothing gets done.

The real rest occurred during the first half of the week when I was seriously tired and needed it. Then the naps, the novel, the change of pace, and even the strolls allowed me to breathe deeply again.

But as the week wore on, the rest wore thin. By the weekend, I was wondering why I existed at all. I stood firmly by as laundry piled up, dishes accumulated in the sink, words did not get written, stories knocked around my brain, and my soul doubted its existence.

God flourished, though. He rested and waited and probably tapped His foot as I went from weary to relaxed to woeful.

My experience as a human being is summed up in the word—unpredictable. The moment I imagine the perfect scene is the moment that the scene won't measure up in reality. God can imagine a leaf and make it quiver with life. I imagine anything and I stop seeing what really is. I stop being present. Alive to what grows and goes all around me.

The beauty of fiction is that it is fiction. I don't actually expect Luxonian aliens to quarrel about the value of the human race with Ingots or Crestas. The fictional world is only a picture of what is real. A painting of a leaf. Not the leaf itself.

Rest is like that. Real rest is a deep imbibing of reality. Allowing the body to slow to a gentler pace, and the heart to beat with a quieter rhythm. It is not dead space. It does not push the universe and all of life aside. On the contrary, it pays deeper attention to what is. God's reality. The created world. The breath of life. Love.

The fast-paced world of to-do lists, chores, and got-to-get-it-done-or-the-world-will-end anxieties, are really far less real than the "real" of rest time. And that's why it is so hard to stay there. Because, in a way, it forces us to re-orientate our souls toward what is real and important. And that is awesome. But exhausting.

Then we need a break from resting, and we get back to work. To our imaginary reality. Our to-do lists and our work-related priorities.

So, the dishes are done, the floor has been swept, the laundry is in the dryer, I finished a story, and I'll start dinner in a bit.

Life is good. Glad I got a rest. Now I'll take it easy and get back to work.

Allow My Soul to Soar
Originally published on The Writings of A. K. Frailey 8/8/2019

There is a nest of swallows right above my porch doorway, high on the south side of the house, just under the eaves. The papa and mama cared for three hatchlings throughout the spring, bringing them tidbits to munch on whenever they were hungry, which seemed like every minute of every day. Each morning, it has been a pleasant entertainment to watch the parents nurture the young ones overhead. The fact that they eat insects only makes the deal sweeter—for me, anyway.

But then, sadly, recently, a car hit one of our oldest cats. It was a tragic event since several of the kids witnessed the accident, and it left an ugly mark on the day. It was no one's fault as the cat got right under the car's tire, and there was no way to stop it from happening. Just one of those terrible things...like a destructive storm or a deadly disease. Hell happens. Even here.

Finally, last night, as the heat of the day finally dropped to a moderate temperature, I sat out and watched the baby swallows join their parents careening about the sky. They flew in bird ecstasy, capering about like sky-born gymnasts. Delight incarnate.

I know perfectly well that the critters around the place only live for a short time. I care for them as well as I can. Even to the point of risking life and limb by hanging hummingbird feeders out the second-story window. Two of our dogs are so old; they can barely shuffle down the road. They try to follow us on our evening walk, and it becomes painful to watch them trying to keep up. I worry that a tractor will hit them. But they stay off the road if we're not on it. They want so much to be with us. So they stagger along.

In the country, it can seem foolish to get attached to animals since we know full well that some critters are raised as food. Pets are a luxury. An illusion sometimes. It is a human decision who lands on the dinner table and who gets fed from the table.

But decide, we must. And our hearts get involved whether we like it or not. I struggled with the irony of critter care and affection until I realized that I'm more steward than owner. I treat each animal well, whether it is a chicken raised for meat, a dog trained for protection, or a cat urged to hunt for mice. Most of our cats and dogs do earn their keep. But not by any monetary standard.

As Beatrix Potter, A. A. Milne, Margery Williams, and other famous authors have taught me, animals do speak to the human spirit. Personally, my life would be much poorer without Peter Rabbit, Tabitha Twitchit, Tigger, Eeyore, and the skin horse.

When I observe a household cat lounging on the porch with one eye following the birds overhead, a dog ambling about the backyard with its tail wagging in silent greeting, the hens pecking at melon rinds thrown out back, and the happy swallows dancing in air, I have to stand in awe of our mighty Creator who makes the sublime so honest and approachable.

After all, who am I to befriend the supremely confident cat, the immodestly enthusiastic hound, and the sky-larking-singing-a-merry-tune birds?

I am humbled by the honor. When tragedy strikes, I bow my head and accept what I cannot change. We are all only here for a short time. When fried chicken feeds my family, I am grateful. When I stroke the thick fur of a pet, I join their gladness. When I hear the hens cackle, I laugh at their ridiculous antics. While I live, I love and nurture where I can, not drawing thick lines between the human and animal kingdom. God has already done that.

I simply admire and allow my soul to soar.

Stars Twinkle in Concert with Darting Fireflies

Originally published on The Writings of A. K. Frailey 8/22/2019

It's that time of the year again. School arrives with all its rigor and tight schedules. The hot summer zigzags toward a mild autumn. Or so I hope. Late summer heralds the joy of cooler temperatures and lightens the weary weight of high humidity and sticky sweat.

Around here, August kicks off the birthday season and tumbles right into the holiday season. Suddenly, there are presents to give and secrets to keep. The joys of life are not completely swallowed up by essays and exams.

I glory in every hint of change, watching with eager eyes as leaves turn from dark green to shades of pink and red, while orange pumpkins and yellow squash form wobbly lines on the porch steps.

It isn't autumn yet. But my imagination offers the next best thing. I can practically feel autumn's coolness playing over my skin even while I inhale the hot smells of drying cornfields. The gritty dust of the road settles for the last time between my toes as I watch caterpillars wriggle their way to wherever they insist they are going. Even though grasshoppers fly in my face and annoy me, I remember Laura Ingalls Wilder's stories about the late summer grasshoppers and luxuriate in the knowledge that they don't arrive in massive clouds anymore and nibble away local farmers' entire crops. At least that's one problem we don't have to deal with.

On Sunday, I took some of the kids to Coffeen Lake in the hopes of catching a cool breeze. Alas, the road was closed to the entrance we normally use, so we had to settle for a smaller section of the lake instead. Since there was a trail nearby, we decided, with true Sunday afternoon "What do we have to lose?" aplomb, we ventured ahead. After running smack into the fifth spider web, with sticky spider prizes attached, I sent my eldest son ahead to clear the path of all entrapments. Good son that he is, he did so without complaint, though I noticed after a bit, he did swing a branch ahead as he went.

Strolling behind, I noticed beautiful leaves along the path. I might have missed them if the spiders had been less diligent about knitting open-air markets on the path. I was surprised at the first crimson delight and astonished by the time I swept up the sixth autumn leaf and then found a perfectly formed acorn with its cap still attached.

Through the week, I have let my eyes linger on their fading, crumpling forms sprawled across my desk, knowing full well that even autumn's glory can't last forever. The north wind will sweep fall's gentle, mellow mood aside as biting cold and white-and-black attitudes force their way to center stage.

This evening, a mosquito bite itches my leg while I watch patterns of leaves rise and fall over a speckled tree trunk. Green leaves hang still and quiet in the evening air. Birds chirp noisily, and my crimson foliage yet more crumpled and dried out, warns me of things to come.

This year has been a collage of joy-filled triumphs and humiliating defeats. My kids have won prizes, graduated from classes, mastered new skills, and suffered the consequences of a world at war with its better self. I have discovered—to my heart-wrenching grief—that hoping for the best doesn't always reflect reality. Some hopes and prayers are not answered as I wish, yet I must plod along life's rugged path even while keeping on the lookout for hope and light. This evening, my spirit is rekindled as I sit under the darkening sky, and stars twinkle in concert with darting fireflies.

There is no perfect season, though autumn will always hold a special place in my heart. Perhaps because it seems so dreadfully honest. Its bittersweet end-of-summer breeze whispers in my ear, reminding me to live not what is now only...but what might be. What should be. What will be... Searing hot summer winds scorch our souls, and winter ice freezes our spirits, but spring and autumn balance the extremes. Each season journeys along by the hand of God. As should I.

What God Has Desired
Originally published on The Writings of A. K. Frailey 9/5/2019

I just finished reading my grandmother's memoirs, and once again, I see the universe from a new perspective. Marie Haggerty had a terrible relationship with many members of her immediate family, but at age seven, she fell in love with Irving McDonald and stayed in love with him all her life. She and Irving brought six children into a world changing faster and more wildly than they could ever have foreseen. And after each adventure—and misadventure—they would kiss before going to sleep. No trial or anxiety could survive that humble nighttime kiss.

I've heard it said, "Love is an action word." But I suspect that might be a bit simplistic. There are times when love lives best in things not done. An angry word not said. A bitter mood not indulged. The silence of waiting for the right moment to deal with a problem. Not following when someone wants to be left alone. Yes, love is shown by our actions; we are known by our fruit. But sometimes, we love best by not reacting, demanding, or repeating compulsive family patterns.

My grandmother lived through a painful childhood, married the love of her life, cared deeply for her children, made enduring friends, painted pictures, and established new homes time and time again. Ironically, the copy of her memoirs I own does not include her final page. It ends without an ending. I know that Irv died on the way back from posting a letter. Dropped dead on the sidewalk. I don't know how my grandmother died. I just know that she died, and my mother lived on. My mother died in her turn, and now I live on. At some point, I will die, and my daughters will live on.

But the snapshot of her life, the sound of her voice in my head as I read the words she typed so long ago, have made a lasting impression upon my soul. But for her, I would not exist today. Her life informed (and in some ways deformed) my mom, who passed her biology and emotional baggage onto me. And so, in turn, my children inherit my physical dispositions and all the lessons learned (and unlearned) that I have experienced.

During this summer, I also read a great number of blogs and books on human relationships. Lots of great advice. But one oft-repeated refrain made me pause. It's meant to release us from carrying other people's burdens, I suppose. "You can't change anyone."

Really?

I went along with the idea until I pondered Christ on the Cross. Then I slammed hard against the redemption of the human race. We're still apes, eh?

On the contrary, I suspect we are always changing people. Forming or deforming everyone around us and ourselves in the process.

I agree that the honeymoon is no place to try to convert your new hubby into a non-smoker. Or that a woman who loves faux fur is likely to appreciate taxidermy because you stuffed a mink in a perfect, statuesque form in her kitchen.

But the truth is, at the end of her days, my mother was a changed woman. But she had known the love of her father and her father's love for her mother. She may have lost her beauty, her strength, and her wit, but she managed to eke out the word "lovely" when she saw her granddaughter. My dad has forgotten all his academic skills, but he remembers each week to say that he loves me.

Perhaps we can't "change" people so much as we can help each other become what God has desired for us.

Love is to will the good of another so that they can accept and return real love. My grandmother, probably because of my grandfather's devotion, willed me a great deal of good through her honest reflections.

    I pray that the same can be said of me someday.

Wisdom Between Them
Originally published on The Writings of A. K. Frailey 9/19/2019

My dad once said, in effect, that a house is like a child that never grows up. Though it does manage to grow old. How true!

When I "discovered" my house on a March 1st morning some 20+ years ago, I knew that it was perfect for us. Don't ask me how I knew. I just knew. Deceptively large inside, far larger than one would guess by looking at it from the outside, and surrounded by trees, which were, in turn, surrounded by farm fields, it symbolized all the pleasant contradictions of life.

My husband had the joyful, though challenging, duty of making it fit for our ever-growing family. After his death, I just had to keep it from tumbling around my ears.

Over the years, I have learned a few secrets. Houses, like their owners, have their own trials and tribulations. Their weak spots. So the pipes run uphill when they are supposed to run down? And the landscape washes every rain shower into our back door?

So, like any decent human being with a certifiable conscience and good sense, I decided to fix things. Sure, my brain told me. Go ahead. Try. See how it works.

Or doesn't.

Apparently, moving the new well pipes to right behind the electrical box was not an act of genius forethought. Snakes liked the fresh holes, though. Someone was happy anyway. And plastic is...well...plastic. It snaps. A lot. Crumbles even. And guess what? New flooring hates to get wet.

I sometimes wonder if I have made as many mistakes with my kids as I have with the house. Since my children are reasonably well-adjusted and manage to hold jobs and move forward in their educational pursuits, I'm not terribly anxious about them. Just wondering why the house is so much harder to please.

Could it be that my lack of carpentry, electrical, plumbing, and basic know-how skills has set me up for failure?

No, I blame my mom. Really it's her fault. You see, under a compulsive, though, I must admit, a very generous assertion that she would never have a baby born on April 1st, my appointed due date, she decided that she would do everything within her power to have me born early. Using every trick in the book, which happened to include jogging around the block to the concern of her neighbors, lighting votive candles at church, and praying to every saint she could think of under the haze of the last trimester of pregnancy, she achieved her goal and gave birth to her sixth child two days early.

And thus, I have lived all my whole life under the delusion that to be on time is to actually be late. I hurry through everything in dread fear of being on time. Heaven forbid!

My children, though most of them arrived early, do not seem to carry this heavy load of urgency. I constantly have to pluck my jaw off the floor when they turn assignments in on time. Not late. Not early. But on time.

So naturally, when it comes to putting a new unassembled shelf together, I skip those dreary, time-consuming instructions and go for it—so as to get the bloody thing done as fast as possible. Of course! That is what time hoarders do. We hurry! Ignore the fact that I have unexplained pieces left over after each assembly project. I just tuck them in the drawer as another of life's quaint mysteries.

There is really no mystery to the fact that I lay down new flooring before I fix the threshold, which seeps water every time it rains. And it's no wonder that the ensuing ripples perplex me. I did everything fast. It should have worked. There is no higher object in life than to get things done fast and efficiently.

Actually, both my mom and my dad had a lot of wisdom between them. If only they saw each other then as I see them now. Mom's spirit of generosity bespoke of a love for her unborn child that any mother might envy. My dad's clear-eyed appraisal bespoke a mind that accepted a homeowner's reality without illusion.

Perhaps it's not the house that needs to grow up…but its owner.

A World of Faces
Originally published on The Writings of A. K. Frailey 10/3/2019

I drive to a nearby town each morning to drop my middle girls at their driver's ed class. This morning, the sun rose gloriously over fields of golden-brown corn and yellow bean plants. A low vaporous mist swirled over the valleys.

As I pass other drivers—there are not many—I glimpse a world of faces. Men, women, brothers, sisters, mothers, fathers, sons and daughters. There is undoubtedly a grandparent or two or even a great-grandparent among the daily lot.

Faces fascinate me. Some people squint against the sun, while others make good use of sunglasses. I've seen people slashing the air as they drive, nodding to something I can't see, wide-eyed, frowning, grinning, laughing, serious, reflecting. All kinds of faces forming all kinds of expressions.

This morning, a young man passed wearing glasses. A firm chin, slicked-back hair, and a dark shirt were obvious. But what caught my attention was his grin.

A pair of doves had fluttered into flight as I turned with the curve of the road, and I knew the sun was coming up over the cornfield. I had wished I could've seen the birds rise into the misty air, but I didn't dare glance back. But I did glance aside at the passing car, and I saw the view from the young man's face as his eyes rose from the road to the sky. His smile told me all I wanted to know.

It was only a glimpse of another person's serenity, but it helped to frame my day. I can't help but be affected by the people around me with names I'll never know and histories I'll never understand. It surprises me how much a perfect stranger can alter my mood or change my mind.

Some people clutch their steering wheels and hunch forward as if they can't get where they are going fast enough. Others rest their hands limply on the top of the steering wheel. Occasionally, someone will lift a hand in salute. Sometimes, I am the one who offers a soft wave.

Traveling along this human journey, I forget at times that I am not alone, that my actions affect everyone around me, even in the simplest ways. A courteous nod to a driver waiting at a four-way stop can make the difference between a dangerous event and a humorous exchange. Turning off my music when stopping at the park and letting others enjoy the bird song makes for a more peaceful environment. Even the detail of easing the perpetual serious expression off my face and replacing it with peaceful serenity makes for a calmer me and—perhaps—a happier world.

Our faces tell us a lot about each other. And ourselves.

Make One Strong
Originally published on The Writings of A. K. Frailey 10/17/2019

A squirrel nearly committed suicide under the wheels of my car the other day. Lucky for it, I wasn't driving. My daughter was. The one just learning to drive. She took us on a slight detour on the shoulder of the road, but she kept us alive, and Mr. Squirrel lived to scramble up another tree.

I often wonder how my kids will react when something unexpectedly horrible happens in their lives. Being a mom, I would like to control the universe well enough so that nothing—in the bad sense—ever happens to shake up their worlds or derail their plans.

In my lifetime, I've heard a lot of different stories involving difficult life challenges. In each case, the people involved lived to tell the tale. They each faced different realities, but in the end, they all had to stare evil in the face. No one avoided being wounded in the process.

Yet, the view from each person's perspective is so different, I have to wonder, why?

Why do some people suffer and later heal, and others relive their pain endlessly, repeating ugly cycles as if they can't get enough of them?

In a conversation with a friend this week, we discussed the influence of music on our psyche. Some music depresses the mind and soul with repetitious complaints, unfulfilled longing, hellish remembrances, or wanton grief. Artwork can do much the same. In reviewing a pop-cultural art gallery recently, I was struck by how many of the drawings, paintings, and sketches depicted grievous death or demonic hauntings. And then, of course, there are modern movies and television offerings, which we imbibe like shipwrecked sailors tossing back strong drink, binging on multiple episodes, and drinking in images faster than our brains can process what is happening.

The difference I found between hope and despair?

Take a guess. It's pretty obvious.

Family and community. Either you have a strong one, or you make one strong.

I have yet to hear anyone share a life story that involved nothing but bliss and happiness. If it isn't a disease, drug addiction, economic hardships, socio-political inequalities, cultural bias, religious differences, or a hundred other possible ways of hurting and being hurt, we humans seem to find some way to dismiss our bliss or ruin joy for others.

Yet, not everyone is miserable. Not everyone gives in to despair. Not everyone hates or hurts back. Not everyone hides out in the shadowed corners of fantasy or drug-induced hallucinations.

I know men and women who have lost beloved children, siblings, and spouses, suffered through cancer, experienced poverty, been misunderstood, lonely, and ignored. But at some point, they decided to get back on their proverbial feet and smile again. Even when there wasn't a whole lot to smile about. They looked for something to be grateful for. They found it. Then they gave it away. They offered their hard-won joy, peace, and goodwill to those around them.

Funny thing is, those people don't spend much time listening to lamentable music, watching characters slip into repeated despair, shooting chemicals into their veins, consuming enough sugar to send an elephant into insulin shock, ranting and raving about life and politics, or painting pictures all in black.

Everyone makes mistakes. Mr. Squirrel nearly ended up as roadkill. Some squirrels do, and vultures don't mind. There are always vultures around happily feasting on someone else's tragedy.

But we can learn. Hopefully, better than our four-footed friends. We may have to ride on the shoulder of the road to save someone or save ourselves. But we can get back on the road; think about where we are going, and how we want to get there.

We may not pick our horrors, but we can decide to relive or release them.

Family and community—either you have a strong one, or you make one strong.

Back to Shore
Originally published on The Writings of A. K. Frailey 10/31/2019

When I was ten, my mom began renting out rooms to foreign students. Over the next eleven years, while I lived at home, I became friends with students from countries all over the world—Japan, China, Taiwan, Singapore, Venezuela, Germany, Palestine, Saudi Arabia, India, and many others. Each man widened my understanding and appreciation of humanity.

One summer, my mom decided that we (the remnant of my family) deserved a little break. A change of pace. So she rented a little place on a lake for a week. Lake Danoon. It was beautiful, and the first real "vacation" I could ever remember. As glad as I was for a chance to enjoy "free time" without the daily grind, I soon realized that our renters made my life far more interesting than it would ever have been without them.

Three of the guys showed up on Saturday, and I remember how glad I was to see them. Not only did I miss our "Hi, how ya doing?" as we passed in the kitchen each day, but I also missed their presence. Their scholastic-obsessed good sense and hardworking example.

I had, in a fatally flawed bit of logic (given my arm strength) tried to row myself out onto the lake in the morning and did nothing but bump up against the shore for an hour. So when Wael, a Lebanese student studying engineering, Ting, a student from Singapore also studying engineering, and Bala, an Indian student, (I have no idea what he was studying, but I knew he was deeply spiritual, making him wise, if not brilliant, in my eyes) showed up, I grabbed my chance and convinced them to get in the boat and head out into the middle of the lake. With me—of course. I was about fifteen at the time and acted like the cajoling little sister who could do no wrong.

We had a great deal of fun.

Until the boat started to leak.

Then the engine died.

No problem, thought I. I have two engineers and a guru. Who cares about a little leak?

They did, apparently. Not one of the three men could swim.

Now that did surprise me. But good sense kicked in, along with engineering skills, and we (they) managed to maneuver the boat back to shore. Safely.

So when the rental guy came over, I explained about the leak and the engine trouble, expecting him to apologize and show some level of gratitude for the fact that my friends not only saved their own lives but the boat as well.

But, no. The rental guy broke into a tirade. For some odd reason, the leak and the engine trouble were our fault. *My* fault.

Being true to my nature, I immediately felt guilty. Not only had I risked innocent lives on a lark, but I had also managed to enrage a boatman. Sheesh. I hardly deserved to live.

Now I had seen these guys deal with all levels of stress during the time they rented with us. Final exams, being away from family, economic hardships, and cultural crises, so I knew how each of them might react when confronted with trouble. I stepped in front of Wael, expecting him to bellow back at the boat guy. But no. He crossed his arms and glared. Then I glanced at Bala, expecting him to offer some consoling wisdom and smooth the fellow's ruffled feathers. But, no. He clasped his hands and stepped aside.

It was Ling, the quiet and most mild-mannered of men, who stepped up and described to the boatman—in a clear and loud voice—the exact disastrous proceedings and with an admonishing finger pointed at me. "And what about her? She could've drowned!" With matching glares, Wael and Bala nodded emphatically. That was the crux of the matter as far as they were concerned.

Without further argument, the boatman apologized and offered to refund the rental payment.

My mom, brother, and I returned home the following week, and life resumed its normal pace. School. Exams. Meals with spicy scents lingering in the kitchen. Cups of hot tea shared at the table. Hot summer days. Freezing winter evenings. Holidays. Ordinary realities.

But all my life, I have remembered those three men's outrage. Not because they got stuck in the middle of a lake in a leaky boat with a kid who couldn't row herself to shore. No. They were outraged because they feared for my life.

And I was the only one who could swim.

What Hope Looks Like
Originally published on The Writings of A. K. Frailey 11/14/2019

It's cold, raining, near dusk, and I'm sitting in the back seat of my car, munching old trail mix. And why on God's earth would I be doing such a thing? To be honest, I'm not rightly sure. Mostly, I'm waiting for two kids who are serving at a dinner inside the church hall. I could be inside, eating spaghetti with everyone else, but I'm not. Not because I don't like spaghetti, or don't like the people, or don't think it's a worthy cause, but simply because I've worked all week, and the idea of sitting with a large group overwhelms my tired spirit.

This week, I have interacted with a fair number of people online. Or through text. I've reconnected with friends I haven't talked to in months and exchanged comments with people I've never actually met in person. It is a strange sort of world we live in. With media hysteria, clickbait, subversive messages, and scams, anyone with an IQ over 10 wants to play it safe. It's exhausting dealing with a world full of suspicion and innuendo. "Connected," yet on some level, we're starving from an absence of real human interactions.

The words faith, hope, and charity swirled around in my head this week. I have faith in God, and I try to show charity wherever I can, but I had to face my inner trauma-drama and admit that I don't often feel a whole lot of hope. Hope seems a lot like trust, and it's hard to trust these days.

But as I slathered dry lock on the base of the house—despite rain forecasts—and then painted the house a nice medium gray to match the siding, and it turned out better than I dared imagine possible (I even got under the porch where spiders skittered about—except for one jumping spider, who made a fatal leap into the paint bucket—yes, it was rather pathetic.) I realized that, apparently, I do have hope. Every time I show even a glimmer of faith that something might work out, I act on hope. Every time I offer the slightest inkling of charity to another person, I embody hope. Granted, the spider didn't make it, but the house will.

When I look at the house, I realize that I have been hoping against hope for years. Planting bushes and trees, knowing that they might not make it, but some always do. Hiring fix-it guys to repair whatever is broken. Over and over again. Painting. Decorating. Improving.

It takes bravery to go into battle against the elements. It takes supernatural courage to go back into battle after you've been beaten time and again by leaking faucets, rain seeping under doors and through the ceiling, icky mold and snapped tiles. But that is what life does. It beats us up, and we have to get back up and try again. Hardest of all, we have to try to hope even when we don't know what hope looks like.

This week, I am pulling up the tiles in the old schoolroom, and then I'm going to do the dry-lock thing and paint the floor and the wall. Maybe I'll decorate the space as a recreational room. So many kids have grown up and are leaving the nest that I have to reinvent our living space. I haven't a clue how to do it.

But I know the broken tiles need to come up. And heck, I can slather paint with the best of 'em. I don't know what I am hoping for in my house, in my human relationships, or in my life, exactly, but I do know that I have some measure of faith, and I try to be charitable. Hope lives inside those two.

Love Alone
Originally published on The Writings of A. K. Frailey 11/28/2019

My daughter showed me a YouTube video recently of a little girl meeting her adoptive parents for the first time. The child, about four, could not have been more adorable. Beyond her innate cuteness, her enthusiasm, her voice quality and mannerisms, which all personified the very best of child-ness, it was her words that rang in my ears long after the video segment fell silent. After a rambling intro, the little girl launched into the core of her happiness: "When I saw you, my heart just fell in love with you."

It's funny how easily those words tripped off the child's tongue. I had to remind myself, she is an orphan. She has lost her parents. God knows how. I had no idea what her life had been like up to that point, but losing both parents isn't usually the direct road to happiness. Losing loved ones doesn't usually make a person more loving.

In fact, it's darn hard for most people to ever say, much less intend, the words, "I love you." Of course, we do use the words in a variety of ways, adding a few extras. "I love you...r spicy chicken." But it's hard to tell someone, perhaps a parent who has rocked us through childhood illnesses but drank a bit too much at holiday parties, a sibling who teased us unmercifully but freely loaned a hundred bucks for car repairs, a lover who understood our dreams but couldn't accept our lifestyle, that we care about them, much less admit that let our hearts fell in love with them. Even when our love isn't so much about "falling into" but rather a slow awakening.

Or an admission of the obvious. "Heck, do you think I'd do your laundry if I didn't...?"

Declaring our love gives another person power. He or she can choose not to respond. Leaving an empty hole where "I love you, too" should have flowed naturally. Or he or she can reject our love outright. Hurt us. Hate us. Make love feel like a curse rather than a blessing.

Perhaps I don't feel enough. Or I feel too much. But in the end, I find that saying the words, "I love you," without expectations but simply because it happens to be true— even when I disagree with that person over politics, religion, and how to properly laminate the floor— is very freeing. I can love even though the other person has bad habits, is an unresponsive jerk or jerkette at times, and, worst of all, might not love me back the way I want them to. My love, like my self-esteem, does not depend upon another person's acceptance. It is a free gift. Even when it stands alone.

The adorable little girl had no idea that she was giving herself the greatest gift she could. As she offered her heart, she became love personified. When Christ admonished the human race to become like little children, I doubt he meant we should toss our vegetables off the dinner plate or elbow our way to the front of the line. I suspect He meant exactly what the little girl meant when she told her new parents that "her heart fell in love with them." She had love to give. And she gave. Freely. Abundantly. She will never love alone.

Tomorrow Is Another Day
Originally published on The Writings of A. K. Frailey 12/13/2019

It was a busy day. Which is very much like saying, "You remember that episode of *Gilligan's Island* where Gilligan does something stupid?"

I adore understatements. And hyperbole.

I rushed through dinner preparation like a speed demon on steroids, hoping that I wasn't stirring shells in with the eggs. Lots of "life hacks" come into play when dinner is expected every day. (No, I wasn't intending to rhyme. It just happens.) In complete honesty, I don't really understand the term *life hacks*. I understand desperation. As in "desperate times call for..."

So, I'm flipping golden (sorta-blackened) pancakes in one frying pan and scrambling eggs in another. With bifocals, this is a lot like trying to spear a fish in turbulent seas. Not that I won't hit anything. Just the chances of hitting a fish rather than an appendage are limited. The fact that the second spill happened when the third kid asked, "Is dinner ready?" was pure coincidence. I assure you I was quite calm, explaining that dinner would either be on the table or on the floor shortly.

Lest you think my day took a wrong turn at dinner. Perish the thought. Let me clarify.

Earlier in the week, I had decided—in a fit of insanity worthy of a Bedlam long-term resident—to paint the basement floor. If I had stuck to that crazy notion, my hair would still be salt and pepper, as it was meant to be by the Creator of the Universe.

But, no.

Once, I painted the floor a pleasing shade of medium gray (not to be confused with the can in the store that says "dark gray" and certainly isn't the same as "medium gray,"...especially after you work hours touching up weak spots with the dark and discovering that your floor looks like it has contracted an Amazonian disease.)

Where the heck was I?

Oh, yes. Hair. So, once I cured the floor of its horrendous look, I stared at the walls, pondering whether my life was still worth living. Of course, the walls couldn't answer. They looked so wretchedly off-color. The smoke smudges from the wood stove should have been some comfort.

But, no.

As I was going to the store anyway... I got what I thought was cream-colored paint. Apparently not. Ever heard of Sahara-Desert-colored paint? Well, now I HAVE.

Painting the walls wasn't hard. Drips are a part of life. When I came to the windowsills, I just choked down a sob since I knew that I could hardly stop now, and I painted everything that wasn't actually made of glass or steel.

In the process, I somehow gave my hair a few highlights that Frankenstein's wife might envy.

This led to a strong desire to take a shower.

Have you ever noticed that the shower cleanser bottle and the shampoo bottle are completely different shapes? There is a reason for that. But when you have soap in your eyes, are trying to get paint out of your hair, and wondering if social services would get involved if you ordered enough pizza to last the rest of the year, you do stupid things.

Thank God the bottles you reach for in blind faith *are* different shapes.

I nearly did a happy dance when I realized that the mouthwash was clear across the room. Where it will STAY.

It's dark now. The kids are fed. Everyone is resting peacefully. Except a dog barking. Only God and some smug owl know why.

It *has* been a busy day. The kids complimented me on both dinner and my paint job. One reason I love them so much. Such dear liars.

But I'll quit for now. After all, tomorrow is another day.

A. K. Frailey

A. K. Frailey has written the historical sci-fi *OldEarth Encounter* series, a contemporary first contact novel, *Last of Her Kind*, the *Newearth* sci-fi series, an *OldTown* series, short story collections, a modern parent's reflection on J. R. R. Tolkien's works in *The Road Goes Ever On: A Christian Journey Through The Lord of the Rings*, personal and introspective *My Road* books, children's books, and a poetry collection.

She taught elementary education in Milwaukee, WI; Chicago, IL; Los Angeles, CA; and Wood River, IL.

She also trained teachers in the Philippines for the Peace Corps and later earned a Master of Fine Arts Degree in Creative Writing for Entertainment from Full Sail University.

Ann homeschooled all her children and currently manages her rural homestead with her family and their numerous critters. In her spare time, she serves as an election judge and secretary/treasurer of her small town's cemetery.

A. K. Frailey Books QR CODES

A. K. Frailey Website

Translated Books Page with Links

A. K. Frailey Interviews Page

A. K. Frailey Amazon Author Page